MARKETING
PRODUCTIVITY
ANALYSIS

PERSPECTIVES IN MARKETING SERIES

Robert D. Buzzell and Frank M. Bass, CONSULTING EDITORS

Howard   *Legal Aspects of Marketing*
Sevin   *Marketing Productivity Analysis*

MARKETING
PRODUCTIVITY
ANALYSIS

CHARLES H. SEVIN

McGRAW-HILL BOOK COMPANY

St. Louis, New York, San Francisco, Toronto, London, Sydney

3456789   BP   9876

MARKETING PRODUCTIVITY ANALYSIS

to my Mother

PREFACE

The title of this book evolved from a somewhat longer one —"Increasing the Productivity of Marketing Operations." But a title that would say more exactly what this short book is would be too long even as a sentence. For example: "How *any* business firm can increase its sales volume or its net profits very substantially, and more than once, by obtaining and using (1) marketing-cost and profitability information and (2) marketing-experimentation information to do a better job of allocating its marketing efforts to the various segments of its business."

One basis for stating that all business firms can increase their marketing productivity in this way is that it has, in the author's knowledge, worked in all firms where it has been tried, even in large and efficiently managed businesses.

A number of case studies are included, demonstrating actual results achieved in increasing marketing productivity by methods outlined above. The cases are based largely on the author's consulting experience as a vice-president of Alderson Associates, as well as his earlier experience with the U.S. Department of Commerce. The case studies are largely in Chapters 4, 5, 6, and 7; other sources of case studies are cited in the references at chapter endings.

The author avoids statements about "maximizing" or "optimizing" marketing productivity, sales volume, or net profits. Rather, the analysis is concerned with improving or increasing these factors. For one thing, it appears to be impossible for a business to achieve such maximization or optimization.

Secondly, expositions of business practice and microeconomic analysis both usually proceed from the assumption that the objective of the individual business firm is to maximize its net profits. Twenty years of management-consulting practice, however, make it clear to the author that this assumption about objectives is naïve and unrealistic; another book, at least, would be necessary to deal adequately with this issue. But no matter what the objectives of the firm, all managements are (or should be) interested in increasing the productivity of their marketing operations, thus favorably affecting such factors as "growth," sales volume, market share, and net profits.

Using the definition of marketing productivity as the sales or profit output per unit of marketing effort, the author thus suggests that any firm can achieve a continuous series of increases in the productivity of its marketing operations. In *Marketing Productivity Analysis* we are concerned with quantitative factors affecting marketing productivity, such as the allocation of marketing efforts to different segments of a firm's markets, rather than with qualitative factors such as "better" selling or advertising.

The two principal quantitative techniques or analytical tools used to achieve increases in marketing productivity are described in Chapters 2, 3, and 8; namely, (1) marketing-cost and profitability analysis and (2) marketing experimentation.

The author has directed the book at both the university student and the businessman. At the university level, it can be used in whole or part in courses in marketing or sales management, wholesaling, retailing, and advertising. In marketing research courses, it will help the student to learn that questionnaires and sample surveys do not by any means comprise the whole of marketing research. Likewise, in cost-accounting courses, exposure to this book will help the student to appreciate that the scope is broader than just unit product costing in the factory.

In the business organization, even in those relatively few firms now practicing what we choose to characterize as the advanced state of the art described in this book, the marketing manager, the marketing researcher, and the controller can all benefit by studying the results achieved by others. The manufacturer, the wholesaler, the retailer, and the advertising agency will find chapters and sections of material of specific interest to them.

References at the ends of the chapters indicate other writing in the field which has been helpful to the author.

Charles H. Sevin

CONTENTS

chapter one

INFORMATION AND MARKETING PRODUCTIVITY

INCREASING MARKETING PRODUCTIVITY

Any business firm can achieve a series of important increases in the productivity of its marketing operations. To do so, it must make a considerable effort to obtain information not generally available to marketing management.

Two truncated examples are summarized here (and discussed in following chapters). A manufacturer distributing direct to retail stores discovered by a marketing-cost and profitability analysis that 46.6 per cent of his accounts were so unprofitable that they were responsible for a net loss amounting to 44 per cent of the company's total net profits. Conversely, the profits from the profitable customers were equal to 144 per cent of the total net operating profit.

A controlled marketing experiment lasting a full year was made. Sales to all small, unprofitable customers in selected territories were made through wholesalers (instead of direct distribution). It was found that changing the channels of distribution to small accounts would increase sales volume by at least 13 per cent and net operating profits by 18 per cent.

Another company discovered that one of its most important products was very unprofitable. It was responsible for a net loss of 14.5 per cent of its substantial sales volume. Advertising expenditures were particularly heavy for this product. It was hypothesized that advertising had been pushed very much beyond the point of sharply diminishing returns. A series of market experiments was carried out for a sufficiently long period of time. This provided a basis for estimating the long-range sales and profit effects of reducing advertising of the product. A 50 per cent reduction in advertising reduced sales volume of the product by something like 2 per cent, while changing the net loss to a substantial dollar net profit contribution.

Before the end of the twentieth century, marketing managers, like military commanders, will probably be utilizing "command-and-control" marketing information systems in arriving at many of their important decisions. As an output of a computer, a large-screen display will graphically portray a series of geometric figures for each of a firm's important products, customer classes, and sales territories. This graphic display will predict with a high degree of accuracy how net profits and/or sales will respond to certain changes in a number of important interacting marketing efforts, e.g., selling, advertising, point-of-purchase displays, etc.

Viewing the graphic display, the marketing manager will make a decision—either to continue in the next time period the *status quo* marketing operations for product X or to change product X's (or other sales segment's) marketing operations in the directions indicated by the geometric figure, with the objective of increasing product X's net profits or sales volume. Six or eight months later the command-and-control system will show a new and up-to-date portion of the response surface for product X, and the marketing manager will repeat his decision-making process.

Rube-Goldbergish and science-fictionish as the above appears to be, many of the essential elements of such a command-and-control marketing information system appear to be technically feasible even now in the present state of the art. These essential elements are discussed in the remaining chapters of this book.

INCREASING PRODUCTIVITY VERSUS MAXIMIZATION

It is generally taken for granted that the attainable goal of the business firm is to maximize its net profits. But it is quite clear that a firm can never really achieve this. For one thing, a business organization rarely makes the prolonged effort to achieve the optimum action in any realistic decision problem because of the enormous complexity involved. There are usually an enormous number of possible choices of action with regard to any one business decision. Any attempt to obtain the necessary information on all the possible alternatives would be self-defeating. Also, business firms, like individuals, are very limited in their ability to foresee the future [1].

"Long-range planning" is becoming more important than in the past, but business organizations still generally use decision rules emphasizing short-run reaction to feedback from the environment rather than trying to anticipate correctly uncertain events in the far-distant future. Thus, "You won't make many friends by questioning top executives closely about their company's long-range goals. Planning can be one of the weakest links in the U.S. Corporation—in fact, 2,900 out of 3,600 U.S. manufacturers with sales of $10 million or more have no formalized system for doing so [2]."

A business organization has been characterized as a coalition of individuals having different goals. Most business organizations, most of the time, exist and thrive under conditions in which a considerable latent conflict of goals is present. Procedures for resolving such conflicts do not necessarily make their goals internally consistent. Also, since the attention to goals in a business organization is sporadic and limited, there is an absence of any strong pressures to resolve internal inconsistencies [3].

A biologist, Ludwig von Bertalanffy, introduced the concept of "open systems." An open system will appear to seek objectives without being in any possible sense of the word "rational." The reason why the open system appears to be goal seeking, although there is no rationality behind it, is that it is so set up that there is equilibrium among its parts. The system will seek to return to equilibrium, or "stasis," every time its equilibrium is disturbed [4].

The business organization, in short, may be characterized as an adaptive open system rather than as an omniscient optimizing system seeking and able to maximize its net profits.

MARKETING DECISIONS IN AN INFORMATION VOID

Most business organizations are multiproduct firms; the typical business, whether that of a manufacturer, wholesaler, or retailer, markets a fairly large number (sometimes several thousands) of differentiated products. In fact, it is hard to think of a firm which markets only one product. Each one of these numerous products of a single firm shares a different market with competing products of other firms. Also, each one of these products requires more than one type of marketing effort; a marketing "mix" of several types of effort is expended on each product. Additionally, business firms generally sell to several different types and size classes of customers, and (except for single-unit retailers) they generally market in a number of different sales territories.

But that part of the total marketing effort of the firm which was expended during any given time period on each product or customer class or sales territory is generally not known. For example, single-product marketing-cost figures now generally available in most firms are patently inaccurate and misleading. Correct and useful determinations of marketing costs and net profit contributions for individual products in the multiproduct firm require sophisticated analytical techniques which are not generally used.

In only a relatively limited number of firms does management know its single-product marketing costs and profits, even

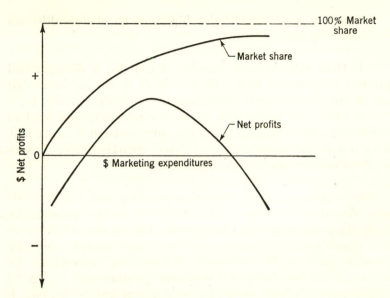

Fig. 1.1   A product's market share and net profits as functions of its marketing expenditures.

at past sales levels. An even smaller number of firms can predict with reasonable accuracy how sales volume and net profits of a single product would vary with changes in the total level or composition of the marketing efforts expended on the product. (This same lack of information also generally prevails with regard to the marketing costs and profits of other segmentations of the total business, such as individual customer classes and sales territories.)

If the marketing expenditures for any single product of a manufacturing firm were to be increased over time from one period to the next, two separate but related phenomena (see Fig. 1.1) would generally be encountered:

1. Sales volume sooner or later would tend to increase at a decreasing rate—flattening out and approaching (but never reaching) 100 per cent of market share as its upper limit.

2. Net profit contributions sooner or later would reach a maximum, then decrease, then become negative.

Together, these two relationships pose an obvious dilemma for marketing management:

1. High sales volume (market share) for a differentiated product may require such a high level of marketing effort that net profits may be much lower than they potentially could be.
2. High net profits may involve a relatively low level of marketing effort. Consequently, the differentiated product may have a low and unstable sales volume (market share) exceedingly vulnerable to competitive pressures.

In reality, of course, marketing planning and decision making proceed in a manner quite different from that suggested by both these oversimplified alternatives. This is not only because the actual market situations are much more complex but also because none of the seemingly rudimentary information involved in the two functional relationships illustrated in Fig. 1.1 is generally available to marketing management [5]. In fact, it is reasonable to say that the following errors usually occur in marketing operations because of the lack of necessary information:

1. *The marketing budget for a single product is too large.* The present level of expenditure results in such sharply diminishing returns that substantial gains would be obtainable through shifting efforts to other products (where the rate of diminishing returns is not so great) .
2. *The marketing budget for a single product is too small.* Either added expenditures would bring increasing returns, or the rate of diminishing returns is still low as compared with that for other products.
3. *The marketing mix is inefficient.* Either not enough or (more likely) too much is being spent, for example, on advertising a product as compared with personal efforts to sell it. Changes in the marketing mix would increase the product's sales or profit contribution dollars.
4. *Marketing efforts are grossly misallocated, as among products, customers, and territories.* If the allocations among prod-

ucts were changed, even though the total level of expenditure remained the same, total sales or net profits would be increased.

This listing is critical of the generally existing kinds (or lack) of marketing information rather than being a criticism of marketing management. Even the fact that a particular decision was followed by a much less than achievable increase in sales or profits is not generally known to marketing management because of the limitations on available information. Conversely, management undoubtedly would make better decisions if better information were available.

CONCENTRATION OF MARKETS

Our economy is still a highly concentrated one, in spite of all movements toward decentralization. More than half the persons in this country live in less than 150 metropolitan areas, which constitute but a very small fraction of the total land area of the continental United States (maybe 4 per cent). Retail and wholesale sales and manufacturing activity are even more geographically concentrated. It has been found that in 1963, nearly half of all retail sales and nearly two-thirds of all wholesale sales were made in only 50 metropolitan areas—pinpoints on the map. In manufacturing approximately 60 per cent of all factory employees were located in about 50 metropolitan industrial areas [6].

The bulk of all markets were found in a relatively few business establishments as well as in a few geographic areas. Less than 9 per cent of the retail stores accounted for almost half the retail business. Similarly, less than 9 per cent of the wholesalers did almost 60 per cent of the wholesale business. A relatively small number of factories produced the bulk of the goods manufactured. Ten per cent of the factories turned out more than 75 per cent of the total value added by manufactures [6].

The markets and sales of the individual business firm show a pattern of concentration which parallels the above pattern of concentration in the economy as a whole. For example, one manufacturer found that 78 per cent of his customers produced only slightly more than 2 per cent of the sales volume. In another business, 48 per cent of the orders accounted for only 5 per cent of the sales. In yet another case, 76 per cent of the number of products manufactured accounted for only 3 per cent of the sales volume. In another business, 59 per cent of the salesmen's calls were made on accounts from which only 12 per cent of the sales were obtained [7].

In a wholesale grocery firm it was found that more than 50 per cent of the total number of customers brought in less than 2 per cent of the total sales volume. Similarly, 40 per cent of the total number of items carried in stock accounted for less than 2 per cent of the total sales volume [7]. Finally, the consumption of many products appears to be concentrated in a relatively small percentage of households. Thus, for example, it appears that only 17 per cent of the households consume 88 per cent of the beer [8].

One result of these patterns of concentration in the markets of the individual firm, as will be shown in the following chapters, is that no company makes all its sales at equal profit. There is some sales volume in every business which is much more profitable than would be indicated by the company-wide net profit ratio. Likewise, there is a sizable proportion of sales transactions in almost every business which are much less profitable than average—or even definitely unprofitable. Where grossly unprofitable segments of the business are revealed, there is an opportunity for significantly improving the over-all productivity of marketing expenditures.

Achievement of one or more of the five kinds of increase in marketing productivity which are outlined in the following section is facilitated by two types of information. The first is the matching of the marketing costs and revenues of segments of the business, such as individual products. This reveals the generally numerous unprofitable segments. Often, this profit (or loss) information by segments is alone sufficient.

Frequently, however, it is also necessary to know what would happen to sales and/or profits if marketing efforts were shifted from one segment to another, as from an unprofitable to a profitable segment. There appears to be only one reliable way of obtaining this second type of information, namely, by means of market experimentation.

THE CONCEPT OF MARKETING PRODUCTIVITY

The concept of productivity or efficiency is borrowed from the subject of mechanics in the science of physics and is defined there as the ratio of effect produced to energy expended. In the present context, marketing productivity refers to the ratio of sales or net profits (effect produced) to marketing costs (energy expended) for a specific segment of the business. Thus, the productivity of marketing operations can be increased in any one of the following five ways:

1. An increase in sales or net profits proportionately greater than a corresponding increase in marketing costs
2. An increase in sales or net profits with the same marketing costs
3. An increase in sales or net profits with a decrease in marketing costs
4. The same sales or net profits with a decrease in marketing costs
5. A decrease in sales or net profits proportionately less than a corresponding decrease in marketing costs

In brief, it appears to be inefficient to run a marketing organization to generate sales and profits only. The marketing operation should also be run so as to generate information that will facilitate increases in marketing productivity.

REFERENCES

1. Richard M. Cyert and James G. March, *A Behavioral Theory of the Firm*, Prentice-Hall, Inc., Englewood Cliffs, N.J., 1963.
2. *Business Week*, New York, June 1, 1963, p. 54.
3. David K. Miller and Martin K. Starr, *Executive Decisions and Operations Research*, Prentice-Hall, Inc., Englewood Cliffs, N.J., 1960, chap. 3.

4. Ludwig von Bertalanffy, *Modern Theories of Development: An Introduction to Theoretical Biology*, Oxford University Press, Fair Lawn, N.J., 1933.
5. Charles H. Sevin, "Measuring the Productivity of Marketing Expenditures," in Wroe Alderson and Stanley J. Shapiro (eds.), *Marketing and the Computer*, Prentice-Hall, Inc., Englewood Cliffs, N.J., 1963, part II, chap. 4.
6. *Statistical Abstract*, U.S. Bureau of the Census, Government Printing Office, Washington, 1963.
7. Charles H. Sevin, *Distribution Cost Analysis*, U.S. Department of Commerce, Government Printing Office, Washington, 1946.
8. Dik Warren Twedt, "How Important to Market Strategy Is the 'Heavy User'" (based on household panel data of the *Chicago Tribune*), *Journal of Marketing*, January, 1964, p. 71.

chapter two

MARKETING-COST AND PROFITABILITY INFORMATION: MANUFACTURING AND WHOLESALING

JUDGMENT METHODS OF ESTIMATING SEGMENTAL MARKETING COSTS

Manufacturers and wholesalers generally do not know reasonably accurately the dollar marketing costs and the dollar profit (or loss) contribution of each of their products, customers, sales territories, and other segments of their business.

In the case of wholesalers, the attempt is generally not even made to obtain this information. It is useful to recall that wholesalers generally stock and sell several thousand different products to a large number of customers. Probably most wholesalers arrive at judgments as to the relative profitability of the various items in their inventory on the basis principally of the product's gross margin percentage.

These judgments are tempered by taking into consideration such factors as the product's sales volume, turnover rate, and estimates of its handling-expense rate.

(In Chapter 3, it is shown that retailers follow somewhat similar practices.) Where actual marketing-cost and profitability analyses have been made in wholesaling establishments, it has been demonstrated that [1, 2, 3, 4, 5]:

1. There are extremely wide variations in the marketing costs and profits (or losses) by segments within a wholesaling firm.

2. Judgment methods of estimating relative profitability by segments are grossly unreliable.

Naturally enough, there is great diversity in the methods by which manufacturers attempt to get marketing costs and profits for segments of their businesses, as for individual products. It appears reasonable, however, to generalize that the following errors in the methods used by manufacturers are widespread: First, marketing costs are generally allocated to individual products, customers, territories, etc., on the basis of their dollar sales volumes. (By contrast with the methods described in the remainder of this chapter, it will be shown that this method is completely erroneous.) Second, general and administrative costs are arbitrarily and erroneously allocated to segments, also on the basis of dollar sales volume. Third, many marketing costs are not allocated at all to segments, not being identified as marketing costs but, rather, being classified otherwise, i.e., as manufacturing or as general and administrative costs.

MARKETING-PROFITABILITY–ANALYSIS METHODS

Manufacturers and wholesalers can reasonably accurately determine their marketing costs and profits for segments—such as individual products, customer types, customer size classes, and sales territories—according to the methods outlined in the remainder of this chapter [6]. These methods are comprised of two principal elements that can be summarized as follows:

1. The marketing expenditures of a particular business, which are usually accounted for on a "natural" expense basis, are reclassified into "functional-cost" groups. These functional-

Table 2.1   Functional-cost groups and bases of allocation

	Basis of allocation		
Functional-cost group	To product groups	To account-size classes	To sales territories
1. Selling—direct costs: Personal calls by salesmen and supervisors on accounts and prospects. Sales salaries, incentive compensation, travel, and other expense	Selling time devoted to each product, as shown by special sales-call reports or other special studies	Number of sales calls times average time per call, as shown by special sales-call reports or other special studies	Direct
2. Selling—indirect costs: Field supervision, field sales-office expense, sales-administration expense, sales-personnel training, sales management. Market research, new-product development, sales statistics, tabulating services, sales accounting	In proportion to direct selling time, or time records by projects	In proportion to direct selling time, or time records by projects	Equal charge for each salesman
3. Advertising: Media costs such as TV, radio, billboards, newspaper, magazine, etc. Advertising production costs; advertising department salaries	Direct; or analysis of space and time by media; other costs in proportion to media costs	Equal charge to each account; or number of ultimate consumers and prospects in each account's trading area	Direct; or analysis of media circulation records

Table 2.1   Functional-cost groups and bases of allocation (*Continued*)

	Basis of allocation		
Functional-cost group	To product groups	To account-size classes	To sales territories
4. Sales promotion: Consumer promotions such as coupons, patches, premiums, etc. Trade promotions such as price allowances, point-of-purchase displays, cooperative advertising, etc.	Direct; or analysis of source records	Direct; or analysis of source records	Direct; or analysis of source records
5. Transportation: Railroad, truck, barge, etc., payments to carriers for delivery of finished goods from plants to warehouses and from warehouses to customers. Traffic department costs	Applicable rates times tonnages	Analysis of sampling of bills of lading	Applicable rates times tonnages
6. Storage and shipping: Storage of finished goods inventories in warehouses. Rent (or equivalent costs), public-warehouse charges, fire insurance and taxes on finished goods inventories, etc. Physical handling, assembling, and loading	Warehouse space occupied by average inventory. Number of shipping units	Number of shipping units	Number of shipping units

Table 2.1   Functional-cost groups and bases of allocation (*Continued*)

	Basis of allocation		
Functional-cost group	*To product groups*	*To account-size classes*	*To sales territories*
out of rail cars, trucks, barges for shipping finished products from warehouses and mills to customers. Labor, equipment, space, and material costs			
7. Order processing: Checking and processing of orders from customers to mills for prices, weights and carload accumulation, shipping dates, coordination with production planning, transmittal to mills, etc. Pricing department. Preparation of customer invoices. Freight accounting. Credit and collection. Handling cash receipts. Provision for bad debts. Salary, supplies, space and equipment costs (teletypes, flexowriters, etc.)	Number of order lines	Number of order lines	Number of order lines

cost groups bring together all the costs associated with each marketing activity, i.e., marketing function, performed by that company.

2. The functional-cost groups are "allocated" to products, customers, territories, and other segments of sales on the basis of measurable factors. These measurable factors or bases of allocation are product, customer, and territory characteristics which bear a "causative" relationship to the total amounts of the functional-cost groups.

Examples of functional-cost groups and bases of allocation are shown in Table 2.1. The methods of marketing-profitability analyses are also described in greater detail in the following two sections of this chapter.

FUNCTIONAL CLASSIFICATIONS*

The functional classification of marketing costs which would be used by any given firm is based on a study of the marketing activities performed by that firm. Most companies, especially those serving wide markets and producing and selling a number of products, have complex marketing organizations and engage in a wide range of marketing activities. Consequently, each company would need to construct its own functional classification to reflect its own marketing activities.

Direct Marketing Costs

The separable or direct marketing expenses associated with a specific segment of sales may, in some firms, constitute a significant proportion of the total marketing costs. This may be especially true of an organization engaging in extensive marketing activities, where separate departments are maintained for selling specific product groups and for soliciting specific customer classes. In such an instance, if the primary-expense accounts are kept in sufficient detail originally, or if provisions are made for subsequent divisions or subclassifications of the primary-expense

* See Appendix for definition of cost terms.

accounts, many marketing expenses may be assigned directly to either a product or a customer class or to a territory, instead of being allocated.

For example, when a single product group is sold through a single sales department to several classes of customers, the classification of the primary accounts by these departments will automatically assign the expense to the product. Likewise, when several product groups are sold through a single sales department to a single customer class, the classification of the primary-expense accounts by sales departments will automatically assign these selling expenses to customers.

Indirect Marketing Costs

Although the proportion of direct marketing costs may frequently be significant, the greater part of a firm's marketing costs are likely to be indirect. To facilitate their allocation to segments, as well as for purposes of expense control, these indirect marketing expenses are classified into functional groups. Usually, the activities performed in any one function will be of the same general kind. Such homogeneity facilitates the assignment of an entire functional-cost group by the use of a single basis of allocation, as will be described in the next section.

It is by no means as easy to classify marketing outlays in terms of functions as it is in terms of the so-called "natural-expense" accounts. The difficulty lies in the fact that many natural-expense accounts relate to the performance of several functions, as, for example, when personnel perform more than one marketing function in the regular routine of their work.

But a natural-expense classification does not permit an allocation of the indirect marketing expenses to individual products, customers, and other sales segments, nor does it provide an adequate basis for measuring efficiency and for controlling expenses. It is thus usually necessary to apportion many natural-expense items as they may appear in the ordinary accounting records among several functional-cost groups, since they relate to more than one functional activity. Where necessary, natural-expense items are divided among functional-cost groups by means of work-measurement study, space measurements, counts, managerial estimates, and other methods.

Fixed versus Variable Costs

The functional-cost groups generally would include mixtures of fixed and variable costs. It is neither feasible nor useful to attempt to make an immutable or hard and fast distinction between fixed and variable marketing costs.

The distinction between fixed and variable marketing costs depends upon a number of factors, such as the size and nature of the particular segment of sales for which costs are being analyzed, the permanency and range of a change in sales volume, the time interval, and the contractual arrangements of a particular business. Thus, in the short run, and with reference to small segments in sales volume, it may be generalized that most marketing expenses are in the nature of fixed costs.

BASES OF ALLOCATION

Responsibility for Marketing Effort

After the indirect costs have been classified by functions, they are allocated to products, customers, territories, and other segments of sales. The method followed is to charge the product or customer (or other segment of sales) with the cost of its or his share of the activity of each functional-cost group, that is, the cost of the portion of the marketing effort for which it or he is "responsible."

Another way of stating this allocation method is to say that the procedure is to determine, for each functional-cost group, the factor which "controls" it, tending to increase or decrease it. As used here, the term control is meant to convey the concept that the total level of the functional cost is determined by the total level of the control factor. In other words, there is a "cause-and-effect" relationship between the factor used as a basis of allocation and the dollar level of the corresponding functional-cost group [7].

For example, a time series covering total number of salesmen's calls and total field selling expenses when plotted as a scatter diagram may exhibit a regular linear relationship (with the slope of the line of relationship at 45 degrees). In such a case, the number of sales calls (rather than sales dollars) would be a reasonable basis for allocating field selling costs to individual customers. Functional-cost groups should not, in general, be allocated to products or customers or territories unless there are such clearly demonstrable and direct relationships between marketing costs and their bases of allocation.

Variable Functional Activity

The logical basis of allocation often becomes evident merely from analysis of the underlying data. Some functional activities vary largely according to certain characteristics of the product and are not greatly affected by customer characteristics. Others vary primarily according to certain customer characteristics regardless of what product is being purchased [8].

For example, the costs involved in the storage of and investment in inventory depend almost solely on the bulk, weight, perishability, and inventory value of the product stored and are affected but little by the customer who buys the product. Similarly, the credit function will usually vary according to the financial integrity and other credit characteristics of customers, with little regard to the nature of the product on which credit was extended.

The relationship among costs and product and customer characteristics is more complicated in the case of other functional-cost groups. There is every combination of customer, product, and territory responsibility for the amounts of the different functional-cost groups.

Partial Allocations

Accordingly, all functional costs are not allocated to products, customers, or territories. For example, storage and inventory investment costs usually would not be allocated to customers, because they would not be affected by short-run changes in the number of customers. Likewise, credit costs usually would not be allocated to products, since they would not be affected by the addition or elimination of products.

That is, those functional marketing costs which vary entirely with customer characteristics should not be allocated to products. Conversely, costs related solely to product characteristics should not be allocated to customers. However, some functional-cost groups would usually be allocated (as parallel operations) to customers and products and territories, as will be explained below.

There are usually several functional costs which are directly influenced by both products and customers. Product characteristics may influence some costs in one way, and customer characteristics may influence them in another. One technique for allocating such costs is to treat them as either product costs or customer costs. Another possible method is to treat these expenses as both product and customer costs. For example, certain functional costs may be allocated first to customers. Then, when product costs are being analyzed, these same cost groups may be allocated on the basis of a controlling product characteristic. In this way, product and customer and territory marketing-cost-and-profit analyses are separate but parallel procedures [9], as illustrated by the three "bases-of-allocation" columns in Table 2.1.

Fixed- and Variable-cost Allocations

It is clear that both fixed and variable marketing costs would be allocated to products, customers, and territories, since, as we have seen, the functional-cost groups comprise mixtures of these two types of costs. The question may arise as to the reasons for allocating so-called "fixed" marketing costs to sales segments (in addition to the fact that there is not an immutable distinction between fixed and variable marketing costs).

It is useful to allocate portions of fixed marketing costs to specific segments of the business because there are nearly always alternative marketing uses for such "pieces" of fixed costs. If it is discovered, for example, that a certain fixed marketing cost earns only x dollars in its present use, it may be possible to shift this marketing capacity to an alternative use that would bring in $2x$ dollars.

ALLOCATION TO PRODUCTS

Allocation bases are suggested below for assigning the more common functional-cost groups to products.

Investment

The product characteristic responsible for the expense of carrying an inventory of finished goods, such as taxes and insurance and interest, is generally its average inventory value. Consequently, this cost may be allocated to each product on the basis of the ratio of its average inventory value to the total average inventory value of all finished goods.

Storage

The product characteristic occasioning storage expenses is the space occupied by the finished goods inventory. Consequently, the measure of any product's portion of the storage expense is its share of the total storage space occupied.

Inventory Control

The variable product activity giving rise to the expenses of this function is the number of postings made to the perpetual-inventory records, i.e., the number of invoice lines. Consequently, this cost is allocated to each product on the basis of its share of the total number of invoice lines.

Order Assembly or Handling

The expense of physically handling merchandise in the order-assembly process is mainly the cost of the time (man-hours) involved. Such factors as size, shape, weight, perishability, or nature of the package are only indirect handling-cost determinants. That is, they affect the time required to handle a single piece of merchandise. Thus, by work-measurement study, a "standard handling unit" may be set up. If the standard handling unit is a case of goods, for example, then barrels, sacks, and other packages may be expressed as multiple or fractional handling units according to their time-of-handling relationship to that of the case of goods (the standard unit). Equipment and supply expenses, as well as wages, are included in the handling-cost group, but since wages are the largest and probably the governing factor of the entire group, the amount of these expenses is added to and distributed with wages.

Packing and Shipping

Where possible, this functional-cost group should be assigned directly to each product group. Thus, the amount of shipping material used by each product group can often be determined by direct measurement. Shipping labor also can often be applied specifically to product groups and subgroups, through labor-time tickets. And the overhead or indirect portion of this expense can be allocated on the direct labor-dollar basis. Where it is not feasible to assign these costs directly, periodic tests should be made of the labor-and-materials cost per ton necessary to ship each product subgroup. The expense of this function can then be prorated to products by multiplying the tonnage of shipments in each product classification by the shipping rate per pound determined through the test. Where weight is not available for any product group, a shipping unit (package, etc.) may be used as a basis for allocating these costs to products.

Transportation

Where common carriers are used, transportation charges should be analyzed from a sampling of freight bills in all territories and an average rate per ton (or hundredweight) computed for each product subgroup. Transportation expense can then be assigned to each product by multiplying the tonnage of shipments by its average rate per ton.

Where the wholesaler or manufacturer makes deliveries by his own trucks, the following method can be used: The wage cost of loading and unloading the truck can be allocated to products on the basis of the number of standard handling units or the number of pieces of merchandise delivered. The actual cost of "rolling the truck"—both truck and wage costs—can be allocated to commodities on the basis of bulk or weight.

Where there are important differences in the transportation costs of a given product to different sales territories, such differences should be reflected, rather than being averaged out.

Selling

Specific-product department selling costs are, of course, assigned directly. Much sales-promotion effort by "full-line" salesmen (particularly in the case of wholesalers) is directed at customers rather than products. Such selling activities thus may vary more with customer characteristics and be only partly affected by product characteristics.

The relative time spent by salesmen in selling each product can be determined by a periodic work-measurement study of a sample of salesmen. Selling costs are then allocated on the basis of the relative amount of salesmen's time spent in promoting each product.

Advertising

Specific-product advertising should be assigned directly. Further allocation should be made directly to product subgroups or lines or individual items advertised on the basis of the cost of space used for each. General institutional advertising that cannot be identified with any product (or customer) would not be allocated at all.

Other advertising and sales-promotion expenditures, such as advertising overhead and artwork, should also be assigned directly or distributed on a job-order basis, where possible. If direct assignment is not feasible, these expenses should be allocated to product (and customer) classes on the basis of relative appropriations or space and other direct advertising expenditures for each classification of sales. Otherwise, if no relationship can be traced, such items of expense should not be allocated.

Order Routine and Billing

These expense groups include the cost of the time spent by salesmen in routine order taking, as distinguished from promotion, as well as the cost of the time spent by office employees in the billing process. The total expense is mainly one of time (wages). The total order-routine time tends to be larger or smaller in accordance with the number of invoice lines processed. Consequently, a product's share of the total order-routine expense function depends on its share of the total number of invoice lines. The office-equipment and -supply expenses associated with the order routine may be added to and distributed with the wages.

Credit and Accounts Receivable

These functions are not directly affected by product characteristics. That is, as far as the individual item is concerned, new products could be added or old ones dropped without affecting the total amount of the credit activity or costs. The aggregate amount of this functional activity is determined entirely by customer characteristics. Consequently, this cost is not allocated to products.

Summary of Product Costing

There are thus certain data which must be known before marketing costs by products can be ascertained. In general, these data are of the following types:

1. The average inventory value of finished goods
2. The amount of storage space occupied by these finished goods inventories
3. The number of times the product is sold, i.e., the number of invoice lines
4. The number of handling units of the product that are sold
5. The weight or number of shipping units sold
6. The proportion of sales time spent in promoting it
7. The cost of the space or time in the various media that were used in advertising it

Each of these factors must be determined separately for each product or product group to be costed. This means that a mass of data must be accumulated.

These product characteristics determine the shares of the corresponding functional-cost groups that are allocated to the product. The actual allocation of costs, in effect, is made by simple proportion. For example, if the average inventory value of product group X is 1/100 of the total average inventory value of all finished products, that group is charged 1/100 of the investment costs for the period. The sum of the shares of the various functional costs which are allocated plus any direct costs is subtracted from the dollar gross margin of the product (in costing products whose prices have previously been established).

The dollar difference indicates the relative profit (or loss) contribution of the product.

The basic procedure is, of course, the same in costing major product groups, subgroups, lines, and individual items or brands. The difference lies mainly in the detail with which product sales and gross margins are classified and the detail with which the functional costs are allocated.

ALLOCATIONS TO CUSTOMERS

The process of allocating marketing costs to customers is fundamentally the same as that of product marketing-cost analysis.

Table 2.2   Functional-cost groups and bases of allocation

Functional-cost group	Basis of allocation	
	To products	To customers
1. Investment	Average inventory value	(Not allocated)
2. Storage	Floor space occupied	(Not allocated)
3. Inventory control	Number of invoice lines	(Not allocated)
4. Order assembly (handling)	Number of standard handling units	Number of invoice lines
5. Packing and shipping	Weight or number of shipping units	Weight or number of shipping units
6. Transportation	Weight or number of shipping units	Weight or number of shipping units
7. Selling	Work-measurement studies	Number of sales calls
8. Advertising	Cost of space, etc., of specific-product advertising	Cost of space, etc., specific-customer advertising
9. Order entry	Number of invoice lines	Number of orders
10. Billing	Number of invoice lines	Number of invoice lines
11. Credit extension	(Not allocated)	Average amount outstanding
12. Accounts receivable	(Not allocated)	Number of invoices posted

As shown in Table 2.2, the functional-cost groups used in costing customers are basically the same as those used in costing products. Not all these cost groups are allocated to customers, however, and the bases of allocation differ somewhat. The bases for allocating the functional-cost groups to customers for a manufacturer or wholesaler are shown in Table 2.1 as well as in the right-hand column of Table 2.2. These bases of allocation are discussed below.

Investment and Storage

These activities usually are only indirectly affected by customer characteristics. It is true, of course, that the costs are related to turnover rates, which depend partly on the rates at which customers purchase a specific product. But many other factors, such as the production policies of the manufacturer (and the purchasing policies of the wholesaler), determine merchandise turnover rates, and these are not related to customer characteristics.

Furthermore, these costs would not ordinarily be allocated to customers, for individual customers could be added or dropped —up to a certain point, of course—without affecting the aggregate amount of investment and storage costs.

Inventory Control

Since the variable activity of inventory control is only remotely, if at all, affected by customer characteristics, in most cases this function would not be allocated to customers. In other words, customers could be added or eliminated—within broad limits, of course—without affecting the aggregate inventory-control expense.

Order Assembly

This function is affected by both customer and product characteristics. Weight, bulk, and perishability are product characteristics affecting the amount of order-assembly costs for which the customer is not responsible unless he purchases only certain particularly weighty, bulky, or perishable commodities. The frequency and size of his orders, however, are characteristics affecting the amount of order-assembly costs for which the customer is wholly responsible.

Thus, if there are no important variations in the kinds of products purchased by different classes of customers, i.e., where all customers purchase substantially the full product line, the number of his invoice lines over a period is the measure of each customer's responsibility for order-assembly cost.

Where some classes of customers purchase only certain products which are particularly weighty, bulky, or otherwise expensive to handle, the number of standard handling units or the number of invoice lines weighted for different classes of products would be a better basis of allocation. The customer who buys products less expensive to handle or who buys less frequently and in larger quantities thus is charged with less handling cost—as a percentage of sales—than the customer in the same class who over a period buys the same volume but more frequently and in smaller amounts. In other words, the latter is assessed a larger handling cost in proportion to the larger number of individual physical handlings of merchandise or more expensive merchandise handling for which he is responsible.

Packing and Shipping

The shipping rates per pound of product multiplied by the corresponding tonnage of shipments in each product subgroup to each customer class can be used to allocate these costs to customers. Or if this is not feasible, an average shipping rate per pound of product or per unit for all products combined multiplied by the tonnage of shipments to customers would give the packing and shipping costs by customer classes.

Transportation

Where possible, transportation charges should be analyzed from a sampling of freight bills by sales territories and assigned directly to customer classes or to individual customers. That is, the territorial rates per ton for major product groups multiplied by the corresponding tonnages delivered to each customer class—or an average territory rate per ton for all products combined multiplied by tonnages delivered to customer classes—can be used to allocate transportation costs to customers.

Where the manufacturer or wholesaler makes deliveries by his own trucks, the following method can be used: Truck-delivery activity and expense vary according to the customer characteristics of delivered-order weight or bulk and frequency of delivery. Where delivered-order weight or bulk and delivery-distance differences are not great, as between customers, the cost of delivery may be charged against individual customers on the basis of number of deliveries. Where only delivery-distance differences, as between customers, are great, the customers can be classified by zones, with costs per delivery weighted by distance. Where both weight or bulk and distance differences are significant, the ton-mile basis may be used. (It is not an easy task, however, to compute ton-miles by customers.)

Selling

Selling expense can be assigned to customers on the basis of the number of sales calls (whether orders are obtained or not). In assigning selling cost to customers on this basis, the view is taken that the time per sales call does not vary significantly as between customers. A more accurate basis would be to make a work-measurement study of a sample of sales calls or to have salesmen keep records of the time spent on each call and to allocate the cost of the actual total selling time to each customer.

Where travel distances, as between customers, are significant, the same classification of customers by zones which is used for weighting cost per delivery by distance probably can be used to establish a similar weighting of cost per salesman's call for salesmen's travel time and expense.

Advertising

Specific-customer-class advertising should be assigned directly to the particular customer classifications involved. General institutional advertising that cannot be identified with any customer class would not be allocated. Other advertising and sales-promotion expenditures, such as advertising overhead and artwork, should also be assigned directly or distributed on a job-order basis, where possible. If direct assignment is not feasible, these expenses should be allocated to customer classes on the basis of relative appropriations or space and other direct advertising expenditures for each classification of sales. Otherwise, if no relationship can be traced, such items of expense should not be allocated.

Order Entry and Billing

The order-routine expenses, like the physical-handling expense, depend on the number of orders and invoice lines, which, as an allocation basis, reflect the customer characteristics of frequency and amount of purchase.

Credit and Accounts Receivable

This expense is the cost of the clerical effort used in recording sales and collections and the financial cost of carrying accounts and making collections. The clerical portion of this expense is allocated on the basis of the number of payments made by customers, and the financial portion varies according to the average amount outstanding.

Summary of Customer Costing

The customer data needed for allocating the functional-cost groups to a customer class or customer are (see Table 2.2) as follows:

1. The number of invoice lines on all orders for the period
2. The weight or number of shipping units of the merchandise bought by the customer
3. The number of sales calls made on the customer
4. The cost of the space or time in the various media used to advertise to the customer class specifically
5. The number of orders placed by the customer
6. The average amount outstanding
7. The number of invoices posted to accounts receivable

Each of these factors would need to be measured for each customer group whose marketing costs and profits are to be determined. (As in the case of products, a mass of data is needed.)

These factors are used in allocating to the customer class a share of the functional-cost groups. The total of the shares of the allocated functional-cost groups plus any direct expenses gives the total customer cost. This cost deducted from the total dollar gross margin received from that customer class during the same period indicates the relative profitability of these customers.

It is possible and useful to management to make cost analyses for various groupings of customers. For example, the results for individual customers may be added together to show sales, gross margins, expenses and relative profits for channels of distribution and accounts classified by volume of purchases.

ALLOCATION TO UNITS OF SALE AND TO TERRITORIES

In general, a marketing-cost analysis by unit of sales is similar to product and customer costing, but it involves a different classification of sales, margins, and costs. Instead of classifying sales by products or customers, the sales, margins, and cost characteristics applying to unit-of-sale groups are determined. The unit of sale may refer to one of the following:

1. Number of units of product per invoice-line extension
2. Dollar value per invoice-line extension
3. Number of invoice lines per order
4. Dollar value of the order

The process of getting costs for the first two unit-of-sale groups, i.e., costs by invoice lines, is in general similar to the process of product costing and profitability analysis. Functional classifications of expenses and bases of allocation are much the same as those used for product costing. The allocation of costs to sales classified by order-size groups—whether order size is measured by dollar value or by number of invoice lines—is generally similar to the process of customer-costing and profitability analysis.

Marketing management is also interested in analyzing marketing costs by territories. In many respects, costs by territories are the simplest ones to analyze. If the company's marketing activities are organized on a territorial basis, with the geographic limits of branches and districts clearly defined, a sufficiently detailed breakdown of the primary-expense accounts and their classification by branches and districts results in a direct assignment of a large proportion of marketing expenses to these territorial units. In some cases, however, it may be necessary to allocate to a territory certain branch and district expenses which are incurred jointly for several salesmen's territories. But even in such instances, there are some functional costs, difficult to allocate to products or customers or units of sale, which can be assigned directly to the sales territory.

IMPLEMENTATION OF DATA REQUIREMENTS

Implementation of the marketing-cost and profitability–analysis procedures described in this chapter (and the following) obviously entails a considerable burden of data collection and analysis. The considerable cost of this additional information is, of course, justified by the important benefits derived from the increased productivity of marketing effort (see Chapters 4 and 5). Further, the risk involved in undertaking a marketing-cost and profitability analysis before the benefits have been demonstrated can be at least reduced. This can be done by at first confining the analysis to a sampling of products, customers, and territories and by making the analyses periodically rather than continuously. Finally, the use of computers frequently (but not always) reduces the data-gathering costs considerably.

REFERENCES

1. Wroe Alderson and Frederick Haag, Jr., *Problems of Wholesale Electrical Goods Distribution,* U.S. Department of Commerce, Government Printing Office, Washington, 1931. (Out of print.)
2. Wroe Alderson and Nelson Miller, *Problems of Wholesale Dry Goods Distribution,* U.S. Department of Commerce, Government Printing Office, Washington, 1930. (Out of print.)
3. Edward J. Carroll, *Wholesale Druggists' Operations,* U.S. Department of Commerce, Government Printing Office, Washington, 1934. (Out of print.)

4. William H. Meserole and Charles H. Sevin, *Effective Grocery Whole-saling,* U.S. Department of Commerce, Government Printing Office, Washington, 1941. (Out of print.)
5. J. W. Millard, *Analyzing Wholesale Distribution Costs,* U.S. Department of Commerce, Government Printing Office, Washington, 1928. (Out of print.)
6. Charles H. Sevin, *Distribution Cost Analysis,* U.S. Department of Commerce, Government Printing Office, Washington, 1946.
7. Charles H. Sevin, "How to Control Your Distribution Costs," in J. K. Lasser (ed.), *Business Management Handbook,* McGraw-Hill Book Company, New York, 1952, chap. 13.
8. Charles H. Sevin, "Distribution and Administrative Cost Analysis," in Wyman P. Fiske and John A. Beckett (eds.), *Industrial Accountant's Handbook,* Prentice-Hall, Inc., Englewood Cliffs, N.J., 1954, chap. 22.
9. Charles H. Sevin, "Controlling Distribution Costs," in L. Doris (ed.), *Corporate Treasurers' and Controllers' Handbook,* Prentice-Hall, Inc., Englewood Cliffs, N.J., 1950.

chapter three

MARKETING - COST AND PROFITABILITY INFORMATION: RETAILING

JUDGMENT METHODS OF ESTIMATING MERCHANDISE-ITEM PROFITABILITY

The techniques by which retailers can determine the profitability of individual merchandise items are discussed in this chapter. Unlike manufacturers and wholesalers, retailers are generally not concerned with marketing-cost and profitability analysis of customers and sales territories. Further, retailers typically do not engage in manufacturing operations within the same business, so that the many troublesome problems of separating marketing from manufacturing costs do not arise. However, because retailers may conduct very small businesses as well as large chains and department stores, special attention must be given to devising simple and practical methods for determining merchandise-item profitability.

The retailer is constantly confronted with questions concerning the relative profitability of individual mer-

chandise items: Shall I add this new item to my line? Of the
various brands of item X that I sell, each with different markup
rates, which is the most profitable? Do I make more money on
nationally advertised brands or on private labels? Is it more profitable to give more shelf space to item A or B? Is it profitable to
raise (or lower) the price on item C? It can be seen that the
answers to these questions are of interest not only to the retailer
but also to the manufacturers and wholesale distributors who sell
to him.

In spite of the importance of these questions, however, retailers in general, both large and small, cannot answer them on
a factual basis. Generally, they do not even know the dollar
sales volumes and dollar gross margins, let alone the operating
costs and net profits or losses attached to each one of the several
thousands of different items sold through each one of their stores.
This lack of information is even true of most large supermarket
chains, which may sell anywhere from 3,000 to 6,000 different
items in a given store, as well as large department stores, which
may sell as many as 100,000 different items. All merchandising
decision making in retailing is necessarily done at the level of
the individual item—e.g., what to buy, display, promote; how to
price, etc. But at the item level, only sales price and per cent
markup rate are readily available to retailers. (Each brand and
each size of each color, etc., of each price line of each type of
product is defined to be a separate merchandise item.)

Markup Rates

Probably most retail merchants base their judgments of merchandise-item profitability on their relative percentage markups.
Many comments are noted in the trade press and elsewhere, for
example, that item A is "unprofitable" because its markup rate
is only 9 per cent, while the average operating-expense ratio for
the store or for the trade is 20 per cent. Likewise, statements
are seen to the effect that A is "more profitable" than B because
it is sold at a markup rate of 20 per cent compared with only 10
per cent for B.

Such judgments of relative profitability can be very misleading. Where actual merchandise-item cost-and-profit studies have
been made in retailing establishments, many items with high

percentage markups are found to be unprofitable, while, vice versa, numerous items with low markup percentages are very profitable.

In one such study, for example, "direct product profits" (i.e., net profit contributions) were determined for sixteen dry-grocery items (by allocations of costs covering both wholesale and retail functions) [1]. The results are shown in Table 3.1. A coffee item earned the second highest direct product profit, i.e., dollar net profit contribution, among these sixteen items, but it was only thirteenth when ranked by its percentage gross margin.

Table 3.1   Sixteen dry-grocery items ranked by dollar direct product profits and per cent gross margin

\$ Direct product profits			% Gross margin*		
Ranking	Item	\$ Direct product profits	Ranking	Item	% Gross margin
1	Soup	402	1	Flavoring	35.9
2	Coffee	262	2	Dietary specialty	26.2
3	Ketchup	155	3	Vinegar	22.9
4	Paper	100	4	Tuna	22.4
5	Flavoring	90	5	Ketchup	21.0
6	Tuna	58	6	Paper	19.5
7	Bar soap	57	7	Dessert	19.5
8	Dessert	46	8	Fruit (canned)	19.5
9	Detergent	34	9	Box soap	19.2
10	Dry soup	29	10	Dry soup	19.1
11	Fruit (canned)	24	11	Soup	18.9
12	Cereal	21	12	Cereal	15.3
13	Dietary specialty	20	13	Coffee	12.3
14	Vinegar	7	14	Detergent	11.9
15	Baby food	− 6	15	Flour	− 8.3
16	Flour	−22	16	Baby food	−10.5

Source: *The Economics of Food Distribution*, McKinsey–General Foods Study, General Foods Corporation, White Plains, N.Y. 1963. Adapted from exhibits 27 and 33.

  * Gross margin percentages were calculated by the author by adding cash discounts to gross margin percentages shown in exhibit 27.

This coffee item would undoubtedly have been judged to be somewhat unprofitable on the basis of a comparison of its gross profit ratio of 12.3 per cent and the retailer's average operating-expense ratio of 14.7 per cent.

Likewise, a canned soup was shown to be the most profitable of the sixteen dry-grocery items costed; yet its gross profit rate of 18.9 per cent ranked only eleventh. A dietary specialty with the second highest gross profit rate of 26.2 per cent and a vinegar item with the third highest gross profit rate of 22.9 per cent would be judged as being very profitable. Yet the cost-analysis studies revealed that on the basis of the actual direct product profit (i.e., dollar net profit contribution), earned by these two items, the dietary specialty ranked only thirteenth and the vinegar only fourteenth.

In the now classic Louisville Grocery Survey [2], net profit contributions were determined for individual brands of a long list of items. The comparison of the profit results with their gross margin rates for seven brands of coffee is shown in Table 3.2. On the basis of profit contributions, brand I is relatively the most profitable, followed by brands G, F, H, and D. Brands E and J are relatively unprofitable. In contrast, reliance on

Table 3.2   Relative profitability of seven brands of packaged coffee

Brand	$ Value of sales	$ Gross margin	$ Profit contribution	Gross margin as % of sales
D	2.75	0.39	0.07	14.2
E	1.00	0.10	−0.08	10.0
F	4.95	0.78	0.57	15.8
G	112.50	6.75	5.87	6.0
H	10.00	0.70	0.27	7.0
I	207.69	39.05	38.35	18.8
J	0.45	0.05	−0.12	11.1

Source: *Merchandising Characteristics of Grocery Store Commodities*, Louisville Grocery Survey, part IIIA, U.S. Department of Commerce, Government Printing Office, Washington, 1932. (Out of print.)

percentage markup rates as a basis for judging profitability would have had entirely different and misleading results. Thus, brands E and J, which have been shown to be actually the least profitable, would have been judged to be relatively profitable, since they carry high percentage markup rates. On the other hand, brand G, which earned the second highest dollar profit contribution—namely, $5.87—would have been judged to be the least profitable brand of coffee in this store, since it has a markup rate of only 6 per cent.

A detailed study was made of the operations of 12 drugstores, in which retail operating costs were allocated to groups of merchandise items. Here, too, it was concluded that judgments of relative profitability that are based on comparisons of item markup rates and average expense ratios can be very misleading. Thus [3]:

> High gross margin rates do not necessarily produce [net] profits. . . . For example, the median gross margin for headache remedies was 32.4 percent of sales, compared with its handling and selling expenses of only 19.1 percent. On the other hand, household proprietaries carried a higher margin of 37.3 percent of sales which, however, was more than offset by an expense rate of 45 percent. Numerous examples in other departments show similar relationships.

The impression also appears to be prevalent that the merchandise item's relative markup rate reflects its relative expense rate. That is, it is believed that, as a result of long experience in judging the relative costs of handling different types of merchandise items, retailers have arrived at markup rates which closely approximate these relative item-handling costs. However, retail prices and, therefore, merchandise-item markup rates are influenced by consumer demand and competition as well as the cost of handling. Further, as we have seen, cost-allocation studies that have been made in retailing reveal no consistent relationship between the customary markup rates of merchandise items and their expense rates.

Merchandise-item–profitability Judgments in Department Stores

Department stores have a long history of comprehensive retail accounting procedures, possibly more highly developed than in any other branch of retailing. Yet the typical department store, like the smaller retailer, does not know the relative net profit or loss contribution of each merchandise item. Perhaps this is not surprising, since the large number of different items (as high as 100,000) in a sizable department store and the variety of ways of handling them (takes, sends, sales from sample, direct delivery from manufacturer, cash, charge account, etc.) have made practical day-to-day item-costing techniques very difficult. Department-store merchants apparently still generally follow the same erroneous percentage-gross-margin bases for judging relative merchandise-item profitability as do other retailers.

Professor Malcolm P. McNair of Harvard listed the following "questionable and faulty practices which have grown up with the present retail accounting system in department stores [4]":

(1) Merchandise managers and buyers . . . have focused on the gross margin percentage and the planned markon percentage as the major operating tools.

(2) The planned markon percentage is used across the board departmentally, with tacit assumption of the applicability of average [departmental] costs to all items in the department.

(3) Practically no attention is paid to differences in the costs generated by particular items.

(4) There is an almost complete disregard of possible elasticities of demand.

(5) No distinction is made between fixed and variable costs.

(6) There is a purely mechanical retailing [i.e., pricing], of orders, using either the manufacturer's suggested retail price or a traditional price line [or gross margin percentage] of the department.

(7) There is a general acceptance of net sales as an appropriate basis of expense allocation, in those cases where expense allocations are made.

(8) Too much confidence is reposed in the final *departmental* net profit percentages after expense allocation.

(9) There is frequent tie-in of the gross margin percentage with the buyer's compensation in such a way as to make the buyer most reluctant to place any orders carrying a lower markon percentage than his planned figure.

(10) In sum, attention is focused on ratios to sales rather than on dollars, and the convenient percentages have become crutches.

Professor McNair summarizes his criticism as follows [4]:

> What retailers must get away from, in our opinion, is (1) the heavy emphasis which this thinking places on department-wide gross margin, particularly in its percentage form, and (2) the fixed habit of looking at departmental expenses, both direct and allocated, as applying across the board to all goods sold in the department.

Turnover Rates

Some merchants base their judgments of the relative profitability of different merchandise items on a comparison of their turnover, instead of their markup rates. For example, an item with an inventory turnover rate two times that of the average rate for the store as a whole is judged to have an expense rate half as great as the average operating-expense ratio. These item expense rates are then compared with their gross-margin rates to estimate relative profitability.

On the turnover basis of judgment, it is assumed that all the expenses of the retailer vary directly with the rate of inventory turnover, or, in effect, with the total dollar value of the average inventory. As will be shown, however, all retail costs do not vary with the average inventory value. It is further assumed that a single merchandise item accumulates certain costs with the passage of time, until, if it stays on the shelves long enough, these costs "eat up" the gross margin and the item becomes progressively more unprofitable. Thus, this assumption implies that the space and capital costs, which are related to turnover, are variable with respect to a single item; that these costs stop accumulating when the item is sold; and that the share of these costs which is allocated to the individual item could be eliminated if that item were dropped.

This is erroneous, since the inventory-carrying expenses are "fixed" costs in relation to a single item. Costs of carrying inventory do, of course, accumulate with the passage of time, but only in the aggregate. The amount of these expenses for a given period of time, such as a month or a year, is the static factor, while the dollar gross margin earned by the item is the dynamic factor. In other words, the expense related to the carrying of a single item for a given period is a fixed expense. This fixed expense will be neither increased if the turnover of the item is stepped up nor eliminated if the item is dropped. Since these are fixed expenses, however, the net profits of the store will be enlarged if the dollar gross margin earned by the merchandise item or by some other item substituted for it in the same shelf space is increased.

Dollar Margins

The objective of improving productivity could therefore be facilitated by ranking the items sold in the store according to their dollar gross margins and, wherever possible, replacing in the same shelf space those bringing in the smallest dollar returns with others earning larger dollar margins. This would be a much better approach than to judge relative profitability on the basis of relative percentage markups or turnover rates.

An example of such a ranking, listing the twenty-five products with the highest dollar gross margins and the twenty-five products with the lowest dollar gross margins in a given supermarket, is shown in Table 3.3. According to this judgment method, eggs with a dollar gross margin of $130.44 are relatively the most profitable item, while frozen lemon juice, with 1 cent of dollar gross margin, is the least profitable item in this supermarket.

There are several instances in Table 3.3 illustrating the misleading results from using gross-margin percentages as indicators of item profitability. Milk had a markup rate of only 9 per cent (nearly the lowest of all items in this table), and yet milk ranked as the seventh most profitable item in this supermarket on the basis of its dollar gross margin. Sauerkraut juice had a very high gross-margin percentage of 40 per cent (twice the store-wide rate of 20 per cent); yet, with only 2 cents of gross profit earned, it was the second item from the bottom on the list of least profitable items [5].

Dollar Margins per Linear Shelf-foot

Another judgment method of estimating item profitability in retail stores uses dollar margins per linear shelf-foot (an even better measure is dollar margins per cubic foot of shelf space). This

Table 3.3   The top and bottom twenty-five-item groups in a supermarket
chain, ranked by weekly dollar gross margin (excluding meat and
produce departments)

Top 25-item groups			Bottom 25-item groups		
Item	$ Margin	% Margin	Item	$ Margin	% Margin
Eggs	130.44	14.0	Bluing	0.29	20.4
Cookies, ice-cream cones	121.40	22.2	Waxed beans, canned	0.25	25.0
Candy, packaged	104.38	27.7	Nail polish	0.20	31.2
Cheese (other than packaged)	95.68	23.8	Dry cleaners	0.20	29.0
Cookies and biscuits	93.02	22.3	Straws	0.19	21.8
Crackers	80.46	24.6	Raspberries, frozen	0.18	19.1
Milk	76.25	9.0	Wheat flour	0.18	12.7
Toilet paper	73.40	21.1	Clotheslines	0.18	48.6
Cereals, cold	72.65	19.0	Foot care, first aid	0.15	34.9
Toothpaste	70.22	31.3	Lime juice, canned	0.12	27.3
Oleomargarine	64.99	16.7	Soap, bar	0.12	8.6
Shelled nuts, unsalted	62.37	24.1	Beef extract, dehydrated	0.11	22.4
Detergents, packaged	60.52	12.3	Pineapple mixes, frozen juice	0.11	23.9
Potato chips	57.53	24.3	Orangeade, frozen	0.11	19.3
Nuts, whole, canned, salted	51.82	22.9	String and twine	0.11	33.3
Ice cream	51.24	24.0	Hand cleaners	0.10	20.4
Shampoo	48.90	40.0	Traps	0.10	35.7
Detergents, liquid	48.11	17.6	Pectins	0.09	14.8
Head, stomach remedies	47.80	32.6	Ice-cream sherbet mix	0.07	15.2
Pickles	46.59	29.6	Eye care, first aid	0.07	31.8
Sugar, granulated	44.60	9.4	Pets' combs, brushes	0.05	29.4
Towels, paper	43.99	21.5	Fish food	0.04	33.3
Pies, fruit	40.88	28.0	Peaches, frozen	0.03	20.0
Spices	40.42	35.0	Sauerkraut juice	0.02	40.0
Shortenings, solid	39.30	16.0	Lemon juice, frozen	0.01	14.3

Source: Progressive Grocer, Colonial Study, Progressive Grocer Publishing Company,
New York, 1963.

Table 3.4   The top twenty-five and bottom twenty-five-item groups in a supermarket chain, ranked by dollar margins per linear shelf-foot

	Top 25-item groups			Bottom 25-item groups	
Item	$ Margin per linear shelf-foot	% Margin	Item	$ Margin per linear shelf-foot	% Margin
Orange juice, frozen	36.91	30.1	Candy, 10-cent	0.20	30.4
			Soap, bar	0.20	8.6
Beef, uncooked, frozen	11.83	22.6	Clothesline	0.20	48.6
Fruit pies, frozen	11.35	28.0	Bluing	0.19	20.4
Turkey dinners, frozen	11.04	27.3	Pets' combs, brushes	0.18	29.4
Broccoli, frozen	9.99	27.1	Mexican prepared foods	0.16	30.6
Cellophane tape	8.88	33.4	Jar lids, rubber	0.16	14.6
Noncarbonated beverages	8.57	23.2	Straws	0.16	21.8
Oven cleaners	8.25	50.2	Consommé	0.15	14.6
Italian foods, frozen	7.80	26.2	Hand cleaners	0.14	20.4
Chicken dinners, frozen	7.48	27.6	Pineapple juice mixes, frozen	0.13	23.9
Cranberries, canned	7.29	21.7	Wheat flour	0.13	12.7
Eggs	7.20	14.0	String and twine	0.12	33.3
Lighter fluid	7.19	44.2	Pectins	0.08	14.8
Mouthwash	6.85	33.0	Fish food	0.08	33.3
Painted-surfaces cleaner	6.66	16.5	Dip mixes	0.08	29.5
Peas, frozen	6.44	27.3	Nail polish	0.08	31.2
Corned beef, canned	6.41	20.1	Ice-cream, sherbet mix	0.07	15.2
Nuts, unsalted	6.23	24.1	Hardware	0.07	28.5
Cakes, frozen	6.21	24.6	Peaches, frozen	0.06	20.0
Pies, frozen custard/cream	6.20	28.8	Sanitary needs	0.06	47.8
Chicken pie, frozen	6.08	26.0	Traps	0.05	35.7
French fried potatoes, frozen	6.07	35.2	Sauerkraut juice	0.05	40.0
Razor blades	5.94	32.2	Cutlery	0.04	33.4
Toothpaste	5.90	31.3	Lemon juice, frozen	0.03	14.3
Mixed vegetables, frozen	5.84	28.5			

Source: Progressive Grocer, *Colonial Study*, Progressive Grocer Publishing Company, New York, 1963.

method focuses attention on one of the most important factors affecting the productivity of self-service supermarkets, namely, the best use of shelf "selling" space.

With this measure of profitability, a ranking of the twenty-five relatively most profitable and the twenty-five least profitable groups of dry-grocery items in a chain of supermarkets [5] is shown in Table 3.4. Frozen orange juice earned $36.91 per linear shelf-foot, while frozen lemon juice was responsible for only $0.03 (3 cents) of gross margin per linear shelf-foot. There obviously is an opportunity for management to use such figures as a basis for improving over-all productivity (see Chapter 4).

METHODS OF ALLOCATING RETAIL COSTS TO MERCHANDISE ITEMS

Fixed Costs in Retailing

Virtually all retailing expenses are fixed costs in relation to the individual item of merchandise. The variable expenses are usually of insignificant proportions. Most of the costs in a retail store, such as rent and wages, are incurred in common for the entire range of merchandise items carried in the store. If any single item out of the thousands in stock were eliminated, practically no retailing expenses would be reduced. Similarly, if a single item were added, total expenses would not be affected. In short, no useful or meaningful separation of fixed and variable retailing costs can be made with regard to one or a few merchandise items—nor is it necessary to attempt such a separation.

Of course, there are important differences between the retailing costs of various items. Some items take longer to sell than others. Bulky, heavy items take longer to place on the shelves. Some items occupy more cubic feet of shelf space; some require a larger investment in inventory. Accordingly, measurements of the amount of fixed retailing capacity (i.e., cost) that is being utilized by any one item are most helpful, because they indicate how much fixed capacity (mostly clerk time and shelf space) could be made available for alternative uses which might increase productivity substantially by bringing in a larger amount of gross-profit dollars than at present.

Underutilization

Another factor that affects retail cost-allocation methods is under-utilization. Important activities or functions in a retail store may, in normal times, be rather consistently underutilized. Such evidence as is available indicates, for example, that in the typical retail store the time of many employees is not utilized to capacity as regards merchandise items. Thus [3]:

> Unoccupied [clerk] time is a significant cost in the retail drug store. Wages for idle time represented from 8.5 to 39.1 percent of total operating expenses, an average of 21 percent of sales . . . much of the unoccupied time in the retail drug store is in the nature of stand-by capacity. . . .

It has been found that 31 per cent of the clerks' time in a stationery store was idle time. In another study, it was reported that 25 per cent of the time of pharmacists in 37 drugstores was idle time. The peak demand for customer service at certain points in the day is a central factor in determining the number of clerks needed, and thus an excess of clerk time may often be available when few customers are in the store.

Further, if selling activity increases sufficiently, the merchant may need to hire additional clerks to handle the peak load, even though there is idle time during slack periods with a lesser number of clerks. But the selling activity which affects the number of sales clerks needed and the degree of utilization of their time is apparently largely determined by customer rather than merchandise-item characteristics. That is, it appears to be difficult to trace any direct connection betwen a relatively small difference in the number of merchandise items carried in a retail store and the number of clerks needed to serve the customers coming into that store.

Capacity Utilization

In contrast to this condition, the facilities for displaying and carrying merchandise in stock are usually being utilized to capacity. This may be illustrated by raising the question: Why doesn't a retailer add some more items that will yield some more gross margin? The retailer is, in fact, constantly besieged to do just that. Up to a point he must follow this course of action, but it is apparent that, somewhere along the line, there are limits to the process.

In the typical retail store, these limits are chiefly imposed by space and capital. While credit is usually available for carrying additional items, most stores work fairly close to the limits of effective display space. In fact, there are indications that many stores carry so many items that they have gone beyond the limits of effective display.

Accordingly, in a simplified cost-and-profitability analysis, the only expenses that would be charged to merchandise items in the typical smaller retail store are the fixed costs involved in the maintenance of and investment in inventory. These are, in the main, rent (or occupancy) and interest expenses. The amount of these fixed costs that is allocated to an item is a measure of the use that item makes of the retailing functions which are being utilized to capacity—use which prevents some other items from being carried in stock.

Item Costing Techniques

A relatively simple method of making a cost analysis in a retail store [6] is as follows:

1. *Selling-space Costs.* For the purpose of allocating space costs, the total store area is divided into two major parts:

    1. Merchandise-display and storage area
    2. Customer and service area

The latter consists of the space normally unoccupied by merchandise, such as aisles and check-out counters, and used by the customers and by employees in serving customers. The cost of the customer and service area is allocated to items as part of the "movement" costs (see below), since the amount of space required for this function depends on customer characteristics, such as the number of customers, number of sales transactions, and customer peak loads. In some stores, this area may occupy as much as 45 per cent of the total store space.

The cost of the remaining area in the store—the space normally devoted to merchandise display and storage—can be allocated to individual items on the basis of the display and storage space occupied by, or reserved for, the maximum inventory of the item.

In supermarkets and similar types of retail stores, the display-space costs can be allocated to individual items on the basis of the cubic or linear feet of shelf space occupied by the item. Mass-display costs can be allocated to items on the basis of the number of square feet of floor space occupied by such displays. Storage-area costs store can be allocated to items or groups of items on the basis of the number of square feet (or cubic feet) occupied by their inventories in storage.

The total cost of the display and storage areas in the store divided by the total number of linear or cubic or square feet devoted to such space gives a cost per foot. This cost is then multiplied by the number of feet of space utilized by the individual item or group of items. For greater refinement, the relative selling values of different shelf and display locations in the store may be reflected in the space costs by a weighting which is established on the basis of experience and judgment. This weighting, however, is a rather difficult process. Space costs include rent—or the equivalent building costs, if the building is owned by the retailer—heat, and light. They also include depreciation of store fixtures and equipment and miscellaneous store-maintenance costs.

2. *Inventory Costs.* These can be allocated to individual items on the basis of their average inventory value. The total inventory costs divided by the total average inventory value gives a cost per dollar of inventory value. This figure multiplied by the average inventory value of the individual item or group of items gives the investment costs, which consist of taxes and insurance on inventory and interest expense.

For greater simplicity, in those cases where the investment costs are very small or where average inventory values of the various items do not differ substantially, the investment costs may be combined with the space costs and allocated together on the basis of space occupied. Or where it is difficult to measure the space occupied by each item and relative inventory values indicate the relative space occupied by different items, the space costs may be combined with the investment costs and allocated together on the basis of average inventory value. Neither of these two procedures, however, would be as accurate as that in which space and investment costs are allocated separately.

3. *Movement Costs.* The costs of customer- and service-area space, as well as clerk time or selling wages and other costs, are allocated to items by taking account of selling-time and handling-time differences. It is necessary to make work-measurement studies or estimates of selling time as the basis for allocating such costs to items. In a supermarket, it would also be necessary to conduct time studies of such nonselling activities as stock replenishment. A count of the number of cases per item would provide a basis for allocating stocking costs. A count or estimate of the average number of units (i.e., cans, packages, etc.) per sales transaction would provide a basis for allocating check-out-counter wages and service-area costs to items.

4. *Direct Costs.* In many kinds of retail stores, some expenses can be charged directly to specific departments, lines, or items. The depreciation, maintenance, and other costs of specialized fixtures and equipment, such as frozen-food cabinets, refrigerators, and coffee mills, can be traced directly to the lines or departments benefited. Special supplies and wrapping materials and taxes and licenses for specific commodities are other examples of direct expenses.

Although these expenses may be relatively minor, they should be charged directly whenever possible. In many cases it may be necessary to make subsequent allocations to determine costs for individual brands or items. For example, although coffee-mill expense is a direct cost of the entire coffee line, it would have to be allocated on the basis of the number of pounds ground to get costs by individual brands.

Relative Profitability

A summary of the functional-cost groups and the bases for allocating them to individual merchandise items in order to determine their relative profitability are shown in Table 3.5.

The total allocated and direct costs of carrying a merchandise item are subtracted from its dollar gross margin. Any excess represents the item's contribution toward the remaining expenses of running the store and is also the measure of the item's relative profitability.

Table 3.5   Functional-cost groups and bases of allocation for simplified retail item costing techniques

Functional-cost group	Basis of allocation
1. Selling-space costs	Cubic feet of shelf, display, and storage space
2. Inventory costs	Average inventory value
3. Movement costs	Number of units, and number of cases sold
4. Sales-volume costs (trading stamps, etc.)	Dollar sales volume

The dollar amount—not a percentage rate—of this excess of margin over cost is the basis for comparison. Those items which show the largest dollar amounts over allocated costs are the most profitable; and, vice versa, items with the smallest excess of dollar gross margin over allocated costs are relatively unprofitable. Some unprofitable items may actually show a negative amount after costs are deducted from margins. Such comparisons can be made for all items in the store, for the items within a single department, for groups of similar commodities, or for different brands of the same product.

FORECASTING MERCHANDISE COSTS AND PROFITS

Department-store Costing

Full-costing of items has been most highly developed in department stores, where there are important differences in the wage cost of selling and handling different items in the same and in different departments. A functional classification of department-store operating costs and bases for allocating these costs to individual items of merchandise within a department is given in Table 3.6.

The full-costing procedure shown in this table would be used for costing transactions after the item has been bought and sold. Merchandise Management Accounting (MMA), however, attempts to forecast the future costs and profits of a merchandise

Table 3.6   Functional-cost groups and bases of allocation for determining merchandise-item costs and profits in department stores

Functional-cost group	Basis of allocation
1. Buying	Average departmental cost per merchandise item purchased ($\times$ number of purchases if more than one)
2. Inward transportation	Direct or per cent of total invoice transportation cost, based on weight, etc.
3. Receiving, checking, marking	Number of units of merchandise handled $\times$ average cost per unit (obtained from work-measurement studies)
4. Accounts payable	Average store-wide cost per purchase invoice line ($\times$ number of invoice lines if more than one)
5. Item advertising and display	Direct
6. Direct selling	Number of units of merchandise sold $\times$ average cost per unit (obtained from work-measurement studies)
7. Delivery	Number of units of merchandise delivered $\times$ average cost per unit (obtained from work-measurement studies)
8. Workroom and alterations	Number of units of merchandise repaired, etc. (as per cent of total units handled by department) $\times$ average cost per alteration
9. Cashiering, inspecting, wrapping	Number of units of merchandise sold $\times$ average cost per unit (obtained from work-measurement studies)
10. Sales audit	Number of units of merchandise sold $\times$ average cost per transaction (obtained from work-measurement studies)
11. Accounts receivable credit	Number of units of merchandise sold $\times$ per cent of number of charge-to-total transactions for department $\times$ average cost per charge transaction (from work-measurement studies)
12. Markdowns, shortages, employee discounts	Direct
13. Merchandise carrying charges	Average inventory value of item of merchandise
14. Occupancy	Number of square feet of selling floor space occupied by item $\times$ departmental cost per square foot

item. A buyer using MMA would try to forecast a merchandise item's retail operating costs, gross margins, and net profit contributions before the item was even bought, let alone sold. Such a forecast would be useful, for a large number of the nonbranded merchandise items handled in a department store are more or less different each time they are bought.

Cost Patterns

It is, of course, most difficult for a department store to determine a merchandise item's retail operating costs and profits in retrospect, let alone to forecast it accurately in advance of purchase. Merchandise Management Accounting seeks to accomplish this by first undertaking actual cost allocations to items in retrospect. Then, on the basis of these retrospective or historical cost studies, all items in a department are grouped into a relatively limited number of categories exhibiting similar "cost patterns" [7].

In making his cost-and-profit forecast for purchasing and pricing purposes, the buyer would proceed as follows: He would use work sheets or charts containing the various cost patterns for his department. He would select a historical cost pattern for an item that appeared similar to the one he is considering purchasing. He would then apply this historical cost pattern in making his cost-and-profit forecast for the new item in arriving at a purchasing decision.

Fixed Occupancy Costs

A distinction is made in MMA between so-called "variable" and "fixed" costs. Only the former are allocated to the merchandise item, while the latter are omitted.

It is, however, particularly important and useful to include the fixed space costs in the allocations to items in department stores. As we have seen, space and inventory carrying capacity limit the number of merchandise items that can be successfully carried in stock and promoted at any one time.

These fixed retailing costs should be allocated to a single merchandise item. They may be viewed as "opportunity" costs, which can be utilized by any one of several alternative merchandise items. That is, the buyer should pose this type of question before making a purchase: Can I earn a larger dollar profit contribution by using X dollars' worth of the store's (or department's) fixed and variable capacity to buy and stock and promote item A or item B or item C or item D?

Variable Markdown and Selling Costs

The intensity of the customer's desire for an item of merchandise has a very definite effect upon two of the largest elements in the department store's costs [8]:

1. Selling effort required
2. The risk of markdowns incurred in handling the item

Retail-price changes or changes in demand for a particular merchandise item might affect its rate of sale substantially so that its actual dollar-and-cent selling cost per unit might be either much larger or only a small portion of the amount calculated in advance on the basis of an MMA-predetermined percentage. A reduced retail price might cause an item to "walk out of the store" with very low selling costs.

Similarly, variations in markdowns due to the changing rate of sales would almost certainly result from variations in the retail selling price of an item. Markdowns are distinctly variable in regard to items, being very high for some merchandise items and almost nonexistent for others. Timing, customer appeal, and quantity of purchase as well as price affect markdown and make difficult an MMA forecast of the amount of markdowns with regard to a particular item of merchandise.

Relationships between Item Costs and Prices

It accordingly appears that accurate forecasts of an item's retailing costs, and therefore of its profit rate, depend on reasonably accurate projections of the item's rate of sale. These, in turn, depend to an important extent upon a forecast of the effect of price on sales. It thus appears that instead of MMA-forecasted item costs being used to set prices, the more meaningful relationship is the other way around.

One critical analysis of MMA points out that it should not be used for price setting, because this procedure ignores demand completely. An overemphasis on forecast costs may tend to lead the buyer away from the missing information that he needs most for the purpose of establishing the most profitable price for an item at the time of its purchase. The buyer should be estimating probable sales volume at each of a series of possible prices and/or each of a series of possible levels of item advertising and sales promotion [8].

REFERENCES

1. *The Economics of Food Distribution,* McKinsey–General Foods Study, General Foods Corporation, White Plains, N.Y., 1963.
2. *Merchandising Characteristics of Grocery Store Commodities,* Louisville Grocery Survey, Part IIIA, U.S. Department of Commerce, Government Printing Office, Washington, 1932. (Out of print.)
3. Orin E. Burley, Albert B. Fisher, Jr., and Robert G. Cox, *Drug Store Operating Costs and Profits,* McGraw-Hill Book Company, New York, 1956, pp. 7 and 8.
4. Malcolm P. McNair and Eleanor G. May, "Pricing for Profit: A Revolutionary Approach to Retail Accounting," *Harvard Business Review,* vol. 35, no. 3, May–June, 1957, p. 108.
5. Progressive Grocer, *Colonial Study,* Progressive Grocer Publishing Company, New York, 1963.
6. Charles H. Sevin, *Distribution Cost Analysis,* U.S. Department of Commerce, Government Printing Office, Washington, 1946.
7. Robert L. Jones (Partner, Arthur Anderson & Co.), "Merchandise Management Accounting in Practice," address before annual convention, National Retail Merchants Association, New York, Jan. 9, 1957.
8. Gordon B. Cross, "A Critical Analysis of Merchandise Management Accounting," *Journal of Retailing,* vol 34, no. 1, Spring, 1958.

chapter four

INCREASING THE PRODUCTIVITY OF ITEMS

SELECTION OF PROFITABLE NEW PRODUCTS

Product Life Cycle

Launching a new product on the market under conditions of rapid technological change and severe competition is like launching an intercontinental ballistic missile. An enormous thrust of power is needed merely to get such missiles off the ground and started on their way. At first they go slowly, then, if successful, rapidly pick up speed. When they reach maximum speed, they are coasting along under much less power than was needed to get them off the ground. Finally, under the influence of irresistible forces, they gradually fall back to earth, at first slowly, then with accelerating speed.

At any one time a company will have for sale a mixture of products in various stages of their growth cycles and with different profit or loss contributions. Some new products at an early stage of the growth cycle

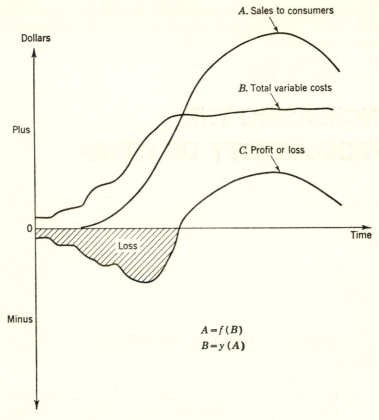

A. Sales to consumers

B. Total variable costs

C. Profit or loss

$$A = f(B)$$
$$B = y(A)$$

Fig. 4.1   Life cycle of a product.

may be temporarily very unprofitable but may offer the greatest potential for growth. Vice versa, other products at present making the largest profit contributions may soon become unprofitable.

Figure 4.1, for example, shows a "life cycle" for a product. One line (*A*) gives the shape of the curve of sales to ultimate consumers, not pipeline sales. The sales curve is comprised of two elements:

1. Rate of sales to new customers
2. Rate of use by old customers

The second curve (*B*) shows the shape of the total variable costs, production plus marketing costs, which are necessary to achieve this sales volume. A more accurate way of stating this is to say that the sales curve has both a "cause" and an "effect" relationship with the cost curve. Finally, the profit or loss curve (*C*) is clearly derived by subtracting the cost from the gross revenue curve (that is, $C = A - B$). Accordingly, differences in the rates of profitability for the various products in a company's line at any one time reflect not only inherent variations in their profitability but also the stage of their life cycle.

Concentration of Profits

In one company, a marketing-cost analysis of products revealed that, out of approximately three hundred items then in the product line, only six were responsible for 58 per cent of the sales volume and 86 per cent of the net operating profit contribution. Moreover, these six most profitable products were old products, the oldest having been on the market over twenty-five years and the most recent having been introduced ten years previously (Table 4.1). All new products introduced in the line during a previous five-year period, however, accounted for only 6 per cent of the total net profits for the company, although they did bring in 23 per cent of the sales volume (Table 4.2).

Table 4.1   Share of sales and net operating profit contributions of six most profitable products (in per cent)

Item	Share of net sales	Share of net operating profit contribution	Years on market
All products	100.0	100.0	
Total, six products	58.0	86.2	
A	20.4	36.6	15
B	13.4	24.1	15
C	3.0	4.3	10
D	2.3	4.0	20
E	12.1	13.1	25
F	6.8	4.1	10

Table 4.2   Share of sales and net operating profits accounted for by new products during a five-year period

Product	Share of net sales	Share of net operating profit	Total marketing costs	Selected marketing costs
	(in % of total)		(in % of net sales)	
All products	100.0	100.0	26.8	19.4
New products:				
1	0.3	−2.1	316.9	281.6
2	0.8	−1.6	138.8	120.1
3	1.4	−1.3	114.5	107.2
4	0.6	0.6	16.0	12.3
5	0.3	0.2	20.7	16.7
6	1.7	0.9	41.8	38.7
7	0.2	0.1	22.7	10.7
8	0.7	−2.0	177.4	143.7
9	0.5	−0.3	61.1	46.4
10	0.5	0.6	19.1	10.1
11	2.6	1.1	40.6	33.8
12	6.8	4.1	32.6	14.4
13	5.3	6.3	39.1	34.6
14	1.3	−0.7	112.4	99.6
Totals	23.0	6.0		

Thus, at first, new products generally contributed more to sales volume than to net profits. Six of these new products were responsible for a combined net loss which amounted to − 8.0 per cent of the total dollar net profits of the firm. On the other hand, the two most profitable new products, products 12 and 13, brought in over 12 per cent of the sales volume and earned 10.4 per cent of the net profit contribution (Table 4.2).

The net profit contribution of the new products studied was low (or even negative) because their costs of selling, advertising, and sales promotion were characteristically very high during the first few periods of their life cycle. However, as sales volume

Table 4.3   Marketing costs and operating profits for three new products (in percentages of net sales)

	Marketing costs		Net profit (loss) contribution	
Product	9 months	15 months	9 months	15 months
3	114.5	17.9	− 38.7	− 0.1
2	138.8	94.1	− 79.7	− 35.0
1	316.9	193.0	−255.0	−131.0

picks up and a new product gains momentum, it very rapidly changes from an unprofitable to a profitable position. This is illustrated by Table 4.3, which shows the changing position of three new products nine and fifteen months after their introduction on the market.

Information Controls

The cost of obtaining a market position for new products in the highly competitive industry on which Table 4.3 is based was so high that, unless a sufficient sales response was relatively quickly forthcoming, the new product could rapidly become exceedingly unprofitable. Therefore, it was necessary to be able to forecast as quickly as possible each new product's probable sales trend in relation to its projected marketing-cost trend.

To use the simile of a missile again, before launching a new product, marketing management needed to be certain that it possessed information "controls" that would enable it to jettison a new product as soon as the product strayed off course. The kinds of information controls that marketing management decided it needed with regard to each new product were outlined as follows:

1. Test marketing to determine the probable demand for the new product at varying price levels
2. A reliable forecast of the sales curve, covering at least the early part of the product's life cycle
3. A forecast of the marketing-cost curve, as well as the pro-

duction-cost curve, and consequently a forecast of the profit curve for the early part of the life cycle

4. A mechanism for quickly obtaining accurate reports of the new product's actual sales to the ultimate consumer (not pipeline sales to distributors)

5. A mechanism for quickly obtaining accurate reports of the new product's actual marketing costs and profits and losses

Predicting Sales of New Products

The company employed a consumer panel to separate the repeat from the initial purchases of ultimate consumers and to observe the developing structure of repeat buying. Knowledge of the fraction of initial consumers who made a second purchase of a new product made it possible to separate the very unsuccessful from the very successful new products at an earlier stage in their life cycle.

As a result of the application of this newly available information to the new products then on the market, it was concluded that new product 1 (see Table 4.2) evidenced only a dubious probability of becoming successful, and its marketing expenditures were cut back sharply. New products 8 and 14 showed clear evidence of being very unsuccessful, and they were withdrawn from the market so as to limit their future losses.

Data for a two-year period after that covered by Table 4.2 showed that the share of net profits accounted for by all new products then in the line (including two additional new products, 15 and 16) had increased from 6 per cent of the total to 11.7 per cent. Also, the sales share of new products had increased slightly from 23 to 24.3 per cent.

ELIMINATION OF UNPROFITABLE PRODUCTS

A manufacturer with twelve products found through a marketing-cost analysis that almost half the total dollar profit contribution of the company was earned by one product, with another 16 per cent each earned by two other products. Together, these three product groups brought in 80.8 per cent of the total profit

Table 4.4   Marketing-profitability analysis
of products

Product	% Total dollar marketing profit contribution
Total, all products	100.0
Profitable products:	
A	49.2
B	15.8
C	15.8
D	11.8
E	7.8
F	4.8
G	4.5
H	3.3
I	1.4
J	*
Subtotal	114.5
Unprofitable products:	
K	− 5.7
L	− 8.8
Subtotal	−14.5

* Less than 0.5 per cent.

contribution. At the other end of the scale, two products were revealed to be unprofitable. Together, these two unprofitable products were responsible for a loss which equaled 14.5 per cent of the company's total profit contribution. This loss amounted to more than a half-million dollars at an annual rate (see Table 4.4). These newly available facts suggested the following specific questions for management consideration:

1. Were products K and L at only a temporarily unprofitable stage in their life cycle? Was there a heavy investment in their advertising expenditures with the objective of getting a return in future sales?

Some light is shed on this question by the data in Table 4.5, showing that advertising expenditures as percentages of sales for the past five years had been decreasing—sharply so in the case of product K.

2. Would the company's total profit contribution be increased if products K and/or L were eliminated from the line entirely? This, in turn, raised the following two questions:

a. Would the variable manufacturing and marketing costs that could be saved by eliminating the two unprofitable products be greater or less than the dollar revenue that would be given up? A rough approximation indicated that the dollar revenue that would be lost exceeded the variable manufacturing and marketing costs that would be saved, so that the company would

Table 4.5   Advertising expenditures
as percentages of net sales

Year	Product L	Product K
5	11.4	6.9
4	9.0	15.0
3	16.8	25.3
2	10.1	22.3
1	14.3	22.5

be better off with, than without, these unprofitable products (particularly if variable costs could be reduced).

b. Could the fixed manufacturing costs utilized by these unprofitable products be used more profitably on other products, or would there be a net increase in idle-machine capacity?

3. Would the total profit contribution be increased if some marketing effort were shifted from unprofitable products K and L to profitable products such as A and B?

Analysis of the marketing-cost data revealed considerable disparity between product selling time and product marketing profit contributions (see Table 4.6). These disparities in turn suggested the following questions:

a. Would total profits be increased if a greater proportion of selling time were spent on trying to expand the sales of product A?

Table 4.6   Comparison of distribution of selling time and marketing profit contribution, by product

Item	% Total dollar marketing profit contribution	% Total selling time
Total, all products	100.0	100.0
Profitable products:		
A	49.2	19.6
B	15.8	3.8
C	15.8	13.7
D	11.8	5.2
E	7.8	4.6
F	4.8	3.0
G	4.5	15.7
H	3.4	3.7
I	1.4	4.5
Subtotal	114.5	73.8
Unprofitable products:		
K	− 5.7	8.8
L	− 8.8	17.4
Subtotals	−14.5	26.2

b. Would total profits be increased if a larger percentage of selling time were shifted to products B and D?

c. Is it profitable to spend 15.7 per cent of the total selling time on product G, since it earns only 4.5 per cent of the profit contribution?

d. Finally, could total profits be increased if some (or all) of the expensive selling effort absorbed by unprofitable products K and L were to be diverted to other profitable products?

A controlled market experiment was undertaken to answer the above questions (more fully described in Chapter 7). The amounts of personal selling effort on profitable product B and unprofitable product L were exactly reversed from their previous levels. The "before" and "after" results of these experiments, which led to a series of permanent changes in the apportionment of marketing efforts to products, are shown in Table 4.7. Thus,

Table 4.7   Results of market experiments that reallocated selling time between two products (in percentages of totals)

Product	Selling time		Profit contribution	
	Before	*After*	*Before*	*After*
B (profitable)	3.8	18.0	15.8	30.8
L (unprofitable)	17.4	3.0	−8.8	0.5
Totals	21.2	21.0	7.0	31.3

shifting selling effort from product L to product B increased their combined net profit contribution substantially, from 7.0 to 31.3 per cent of total company profits.

Large Part of Product Line Unprofitable

In another company, more than two-thirds of the total number of products in the product line (635 out of 875 products) were found to be unprofitable. The loss was equal to 14.9 per cent of the total company profits (see Table 4.8). A detailed analysis of operations revealed no important opportunities for reducing costs and for thus converting the unprofitable items into profitable ones. Management was uncertain as to whether withdrawal of all marketing efforts from the unprofitable products would improve the situation or make it worse.

Table 4.8   Marketing-cost analysis of profitable and unprofitable products (in percentages of totals)

Product	Number of products	Sales	Gross profit	Marketing costs	Profit or loss
Grand total, all products	875	100.0	100.0	100.0	100.0
Top profitable products	41	63.5	65.1	27.9	88.9
All other profitable products	199	23.9	23.5	19.5	26.0
Unprofitable products	635	12.6	11.4	52.5	−14.9

Retention versus Elimination

It was felt by some members of marketing management that all the unprofitable items should be kept in the line. It was argued that their retention was necessary to round out the company's line to satisfy customers or distributors and to prevent competitors from "getting their foot in the door." The potential losses that would be incurred by having a "hole" in the product line would be greater than the actual losses incurred by keeping the unprofitable items. Finally, the company was striving to attain or maintain a position of industry leadership, and the industry leader is ordinarily expected to carry a full line.

Other members of marketing management argued, on the other hand, that most or all of these unprofitable items should be eliminated. Many instances were cited of a profitable item constituting a close substitute for an unprofitable one. The opinions of customers were quoted, according to which certain unprofitable products were not regarded as being substantially "different from" or "better than" similar profitable items in the product line.

Marketing management finally decided to run a series of controlled market experiments, as a result of which 592 out of the 635 unprofitable products were eliminated (see Chapter 7). Long-run sales volume was increased and marketing costs were reduced substantially, while the dollar net profit contribution was increased by almost 24 per cent.

RETAIL MERCHANDISE ITEMS

A relatively large number of merchandise items in the typical retail store are unprofitable. Accordingly, there are opportunities for substantial increases in sales volume and net profits if merchandising efforts are shifted from the unprofitable merchandise items to the profitable. In self-service stores, the most productive shifting of merchandising effort is the reallocation of shelf and display space. Such shifts can increase dollar sales and gross margins with no increase in operating expense and thus produce an increase in dollar net profits [1].

Testing Influence of Space Allocation

In one large regional chain, several tests demonstrated the great influence of space allocation on sales [2]. Thus, in one instance, the number of shelf "facings" of two brands of an item were rearranged. Brand A, with fewer sales, was reduced from ten to five facings, while brand B, with more sales, was increased from five to eight facings. The combined sales for both brands then increased by 19 per cent (Table 4.9).

To measure the effect of eye-level, waist-level, and floor-level shelf position on sales, products of varying size, kind, and degree of acceptance were changed from their "normal" shelf position in one of the chain stores to an alternative position for a two-week period. One-pound-size packages of raisins, which had been selling 66 units a week in a floor-level position, jumped to 110 units a week by being shifted to an eye-level position. A package of pinto beans doubled its sale after a similar position shift. The reverse occurred when a can of peas was given a floor-shelf position after having been on the top shelf: the forty-one units usually sold on the top shelf declined to nine units at the floor level. For all items which were changed to a floor-level from an eye-level position, the average increase in unit sales was 78 per cent (Table 4.10).

Another test showed the influence of fully-stocked shelves on grocery-item sales. The stock on each shelf section for seven

Table 4.9   Influence of number of shelf facings on unit sales of two brands of a supermarket item

Experimental tests	Brand A		Brand B		Totals	
	Number of shelf facings	Unit sales	Number of shelf facings	Unit sales	Number of shelf facings	Unit sales
Before	10	30	5	60	15	90
After	5	32	8	75	13	107
Change	−5	+2	+3	+15	−2	+17

Source: Progressive Grocer, *Colonial Study*, Progressive Grocer Publishing Company, New York, 1963.

Table 4.10   Influence of shelf position on unit sales of supermarket items

Better shelf position	% Change in unit sales	Inferior shelf position	% Change in unit sales
Floor level to eye level	+78	Eye level to floor level	−32
Waist level to eye level	+63	Eye level to waist level	−20
Floor level to waist level	+34	Waist level to floor level	−40

Source: Progressive Grocer, *Colonial Study,* Progressive Grocer Publishing Company, New York, 1963.

product groups was maintained at maximum "full-shelf" condition throughout a two-week period. Out-of-stocks and understocked shelf conditions were eliminated or miminized, and product visibility for a given amount of shelf space was maximized. This intense clerical stocking activity if carried out in all sections of the store would have raised shelf-stocking costs. But the concentrated effort on a few randomly selected products increased their sales and dollar gross margins by 23 per cent (Table 4.11).

Table 4.11   Influence of fully stocked shelves on supermarket-item sales (sales for two-week period)

Item	$ Sales		$ Margin		% Change
	Normal shelf	Full shelf	Normal shelf	Full shelf	
All products	567.50	696.34	153.04	187.59	+23
Peanut butter	98.90	118.34	23.13	26.96	+16
Corn	97.91	111.23	27.11	30.74	+13
Catsup	57.07	75.77	16.40	21.88	+33
Scouring powder	35.01	42.47	5.90	7.07	+20
Facial tissue	75.19	90.03	19.95	23.93	+20
Toothpaste	107.87	140.25	37.23	48.34	+30
Bleach	95.55	118.36	23.32	28.67	+23

Source: Progressive Grocer, *Colonial Study,* Progressive Grocer Publishing Company, New York, 1963.

Testing Effects of Extensive Space Changes

In another supermarket chain, dollar sales and dollar gross margins were measured in detail in a number of individual stores for two eight-week periods. The first eight-week period was before and the second eight-week period was after extensive changes in space allocations were made [3]. During an interim period of several weeks, among other changes, the grocery departments in these stores were rearranged, and the number of facings for each item was changed on the basis of newly available information on its sales history. Also, new lines of merchandise were introduced to occupy the space that was freed when less space was given to a number of items because of their smaller relative sales.

The changed space allocations increased average productivity in these five supermarkets substantially. Total dollar grocery sales rose better than 7 per cent, dollar gross margins rose by 10.3 per cent, and total grocery net operating profits as a percentage of sales rose by 28.6 per cent (Table 4.12).

Table 4.12   Influence of reallocation of space on productivity in a supermarket (eight weeks' sales)

Item	Before	After	% Change
Grocery,* lin ft of display	596	519	−12.9
General merchandise, lin ft of display	78	107	+37.2
Grocery sales per sq ft, $	3.71	3.98	+ 7.3
Special display positions	16	25	+56.3
Grocery unit sales, number	46,939	49,856	+ 6.2
Grocery dollar sales	15,227	16,345	+ 7.3
Grocery dollar margin	2,978	3,285	+10.3
Grocery operating expense, % of sales	14.6	13.8	− 5.5
Grocery net profit,† % of sales	4.9	6.3	+28.6

Source: Progressive Grocer, *The Dillon Study*, Progressive Grocer Publishing Company, New York, 1960.

* Excluding nonfoods.

† Before taxes.

Analysis of Unprofitable Items

In yet another supermarket chain a detailed cost-and-profitability analysis was made of all items in the dry-grocery and nonfood departments, covering one week's operations in several stores in the chain (Table 4.13). The 4,768 different items carried in stock in these departments first were ranked according to their dollar gross margin for that week. A cost analysis then showed that the bottom-ranked 1,568 items, almost one-third of the total number of items in the store, were unprofitable. These 1,568 unprofitable merchandise items accounted for only 5.6 per cent of the total dollar gross margin; yet they occupied 18.2 per cent of the total dry-grocery and nonfood shelf space—some of it choice locations at eye-level height. These unprofitable items were responsible for a negative profit contribution, i.e., a loss, which amounted to 11.7 per cent of the dry-grocery and nonfood departments' total net profit contribution.

Table 4.13   Profitability analysis of merchandise items in a supermarket chain* (in percentages of totals)

Items ranked by $ gross margins per week	Number of items	Shelf space occupied	$ Gross margin	$ Net profit contribution
1–100	2.0	4.1	18.4	31.2
101–300	4.2	6.3	16.1	26.7
301–600	6.3	7.7	14.8	24.2
601–1,000	8.4	12.4	13.6	15.8
1,001–1,500	10.5	16.2	11.7	9.8
1,501–2,200	14.7	17.6	10.2	3.3
2,201–3,200	21.0	17.5	9.6	0.7
3,201–4,768	32.9	18.2	5.6	−11.7
Totals	100.0	100.0	100.0	100.0
Number of items and dollar margins	(4,768)		($4,685)	

* Each brand and each size of each color, etc. (as in toilet tissue), of each type of product is defined to be an item.

Data cover one week's operations in several stores of the chain.

Table 4.14   Average weekly dollar gross margins and space allocated to coffee items in a supermarket

Number of coffee items, ranked by $ gross margin	Gross margin			Space occupied	
	$ per week	% of total	Cumulative %	% of total	Cumulative %
Total, 45 items*	65.18	100.0		100.0	
1–5	25.09	38.5	38.5	12	12
6–10	15.06	23.1	61.6	12	24
11–15	9.95	15.3	76.9	16	40
16–20	6.02	9.2	86.1	17	57
21–30	5.04	7.7	93.8	18	75
31–45†	4.02	6.2	100.0	25	100

* Counting each size and brand as an item.
† Unprofitable items.

On the other hand, the 100 items which ranked first in terms of dollar gross margins generally were the most profitable items. They occupied only 4.1 per cent of the shelf space although they were responsible for 18.4 per cent of the dollar gross margin and 31.2 per cent of the total dollar net profit contribution.

The above-described conditions for the dry-grocery and non-food departments as a whole were also found to hold for most of a large number of individual product groups that were similarly analyzed. Thus, out of a total of forty-five different regular coffee items, the fifteen items with the smallest dollar gross margin per item were shown to be unprofitable (see Table 4.14).

Elimination of Unprofitable Items

Management then selected ten products for the purpose of running a series of controlled experiments to determine the effects of eliminating unprofitable merchandise items. The shelf space thus made available could then be used to:

1. Increase the shelf space for profitable grocery items and/or
2. Add profitable new nonfood items

The results of these experiments (described in Chapter 7) indicated that the dollar net profits of the supermarket would be increased by at least 10 to 12 per cent by eliminating the unprofitable merchandise items.

Improving Productivity in Department Stores

An analysis of individual merchandise items in one of the most profitable departments of a particular department store (i.e., the corsets and brassières department) revealed that even here there were some unprofitable items. (An "item" was defined as a particular style of a specific source in a given price line.) Item 1, the most profitable, earned a dollar profit contribution of $392, while item Z at the other end of the scale was responsible for a net loss of $88 (Table 4.15). Item 2 had the lowest gross-margin

Table 4.15   Item* net profit contributions of the corsets and brassières department in a department store

Item	$ Profit contribution	% Profit contribution, net sales	% Gross margin, net sales
Departmental average:		26.5	45.1
Item 1	392	18.5	33.5
Item 2	242	15.4	29.4
Item 3	145	21.5	40.1
Item 4	100	22.3	42.3
Item 5	58	22.2	39.8
Item 6	47	22.7	36.7
Item 7	34	25.3	42.3
Item 8	29	19.8	32.6
.	.	.	.
.	.	.	.
.	.	.	.
Item U	7	28.1	45.6
Item V	− 6	−0.2	45.2
Item W	−22	−0.4	36.6
Item X	−24	−0.3	56.3
Item Y	−56	−7.6	49.8
Item Z	−88	−5.7	45.4

* An item is one style, etc., of one source of supply in a given price line.

rate as a per cent of net sales of any of the items shown (29.4 per cent), and yet it earned the second highest profit contribution of $242. Conversely, item X had the highest gross-margin rate of 56.3 per cent of sales, and yet it was the third most unprofitable item, with a net loss of $24.

The management of the department used this item-profitability information to make several changes in operations, such as changes in selling emphasis by the sales clerks and changes in displays, advertising, and pricing. Also, some of the most unprofitable items were eliminated entirely. As a result of all these changes, the percentage increase of this department's profit contribution in the following period was substantially greater than that of the store as a whole or of any other department in the store.

Item-profitability Analysis

A merchandise manager of The J. L. Hudson Company made the following comments about how item-profitability analysis has helped to increase his store's total net profits [4]:

> Based on figures of item profitability our buyers know which items, brands, and categories to promote and develop. Together with our operations personnel we start action to improve the profitability of those showing a loss. . . .
>
> With reference to profitability, it has been most pleasing, each succeeding year, to see improvements. We have moved many items and categories from "red ink" into a substantial controllable profit. . . .
>
> Regarding sales, when we compare category by category, our four year record in units to four year national figures, we find ourselves far, far out in front in terms of a rate of growth. In units and in dollars, we have made substantial gains in our share of our own metropolitan market. . . .

REFERENCES

1. Keith Cox, "The Responsiveness of Food Sales to Supermarket Shelf Space Changes," *Journal of Marketing Research,* vol. 1, no. 2, May, 1964, p. 63.

2. Progressive Grocer, *Colonial Study,* Progressive Grocer Publishing Company, New York, 1963.
3. Progressive Grocer, *The Dillon Study,* Progressive Grocer Publishing Company, New York, 1960.
4. Carl F. Beier, "Merchandise Management Accounting's Impact on Decision Making," address at the Ninth Annual Home Furnishing Conference, National Retail Merchants Association, New York, Apr. 3, 1963.

chapter five

INCREASING THE PRODUCTIVITY OF CUSTOMERS AND TERRITORIES

UNPROFITABLE CUSTOMERS

Alternative Solutions for Unprofitable Customers

A certain manufacturer distributed a long product line (with relatively low average value per invoice line) through company branches direct to retail stores throughout the United States. A marketing-cost analysis showed that almost half of all his accounts were unprofitable. These unprofitable customers were responsible for a net loss amounting to 44 per cent of the company's final realized profits. In other words, the profits from the profitable customers were 144 per cent of the company's net profit as shown on the operating statement (see Table 5.1). Some of the principal alternatives considered with regard to unprofitable customers were these:

1. Shifting some selling effort from unprofitable to profitable accounts

72

Table 5.1   Marketing-cost analysis of profitable and unprofitable customers (in percentages)

	All customers	Profitable customers	Unprofitable customers
Number of customers	100	53.4	46.6
$ Sales volume	100	89.4	10.6
$ Gross profit	100	89.8	10.2
$ Marketing costs	100	54.6	45.4
$ Marketing profit (or loss)	100	144.0	−44.0

2. Changing the pricing and discount structure so as to increase the prices charged to unprofitable customers

3. Changing the channels of distribution so as to serve the unprofitable customers through wholesalers or on a mail-order basis

4. Eliminating the unprofitable customers

Shifting effort

In this company approximately 50 per cent of total selling time (exclusive of traveling, etc.) was spent on unprofitable accounts. In other words, if salesmen need not call on these unprofitable accounts, then 50 per cent of their selling time would be made available for other uses. For example, the salesmen could spend more time in calling on the larger profitable accounts. Redirecting the efforts of the sales force would be equivalent to a large increase in the total number of salesmen. A similarly large proportion of the fixed costs involved in order-filling and billing capacity in the branches would likewise be made available for alternative uses if the large number of small unprofitable accounts were handled differently.

Accordingly, marketing management needed to know:

1. The increased future sales likely to result if more sales calls were made on each type of profitable customer

2. The effect on future sales if fewer sales calls were made on each type of unprofitable account

Increasing Prices

Another alternative would be to increase the prices charged to unprofitable customers. The marketing-cost rates for the unprofitable customers appeared to be so high, however, that, at best, increased prices to unprofitable accounts probably would serve to recoup only part of the losses. There were, of course, a number of ways by which this alternative could be implemented, such as:

1. Imposing a service charge on each total order (or invoice) below a certain minimum order size

2. Raising prices on individual products when less than a certain number of units was purchased in a single order (of course these two methods would affect large as well as small accounts)

3. Raising prices on all products purchased by accounts whose total volume of purchases for the preceding year was less than a certain amount (such as, say, $1,000 or $500) *

Changing Distribution Channels

A third alternative would be to turn over small unprofitable accounts to wholesale distributors. Even if the company gave the wholesaler an additional discount so that the small retailer would pay the same price as under direct distribution, the company might still be ahead because of the very substantial loss involved in selling direct.

Another possibility would be to stop sales calls on the small unprofitable accounts. Their business might be solicited and orders handled on a mail-order basis. They could be sent catalogues and promotional literature through the mails, and their orders could be returned to the company by mail.

The company might risk losing some sales volume from these small unprofitable accounts if they were turned over to

---

* Substantial price or quantity discount differentials between small and larger customers can easily be justified on the basis of the very large marketing-cost differentials between profitable and unprofitable accounts that are revealed by a marketing-cost analysis. Such cost justifications are required by the Robinson-Patman Act.

wholesale distributors or served on a mail-order basis. However, since approximately half of the salesmen's selling time could be made available for more calls on profitable accounts, it appeared that, if anything, the total sales volume of the company would be increased rather than decreased.

Eliminating Unprofitable Accounts

A final alternative would be to stop serving the unprofitable accounts. A large proportion of such accounts might be outlets with small total volume, buying low-margin products, possibly not well managed, etc. Also many might be located in the same retail trading areas as some of the profitable retail accounts, so that consumers might well go to the profitable stores if they no longer found the company's products in the unprofitable outlets.

Marketing Experiments

In order to get reliable information on the effects of these alternatives as a basis for a decision, management decided to run a series of controlled marketing experiments. In one set of territories, all small unprofitable customers were served on a mail-order basis, while in another group of territories they were handled by wholesale distributors. (For a fuller description of these experiments, see Chapter 7.) At the end of a year, the following results were obtained:

	% Net increase	
	Sales	Net profit contribution
Mail order	+10.8	+ 9.5
Wholesale distributors	+13.0	+28.1

On the basis of these results, management decided to turn over all small unprofitable accounts to wholesale distributors, thereby achieving a substantial increase in the productivity of marketing operations.

Fixed and Variable Customer Costs

Another manufacturer also found that he had a large number of unprofitable accounts. As a result, one entire channel of distribution was discontinued, small customers in a second channel were eliminated, while sales pressure on the remaining, profitable customers was increased. After only one year, net profits doubled.

The results of customer-cost analyses are shown in part *A* of Table 5.2. Cost analysis confirmed what had been suspected for some time, namely, that customers in channel C were, on the whole, unprofitable, though management had not been fully aware of this. Sales to channel C customers barely covered out-of-pocket costs, leaving nothing for fixed costs or for net profit. The results were no better when these cost trends were projected to a higher sales volume while they were even worse at lower levels of volume. Moreover, even in a year of very high sales volume, the total revenue from channel D was actually less than out-of-pocket costs.

The planned changes in channels of distribution called for an increase in net profits by eliminating losses from unprofitable channels C and D. But the elimination of unprofitable sales would leave idle manufacturing and marketing capacity. Therefore, the next step was to utilize this idle capacity by increasing sales pressure on the profitable accounts in channels A, B, and C. Of course, this increase in sales could not be accomplished immediately, and it could not be obtained without added out-of-pocket expenditure for sales promotion.

As a result of all these changes, it was planned that there would be an increase in net profits in the first year, as summarized in part *B* of Table 5.2. The results of actual operations varied somewhat from this plan, since there were many other factors operating to influence the results, some favorable, and some unfavorable. However, the net results as shown in part *C* of Table 5.2 were even better than expected; net profits were approximately doubled [1].

Change to Direct Distribution

Yet another company used wholesale dealers to distribute a line of high-value technical products requiring sales engineering

Table 5.2   Sales, variable costs, and profit margins by channels
of distribution

A. Before Changes in Channels

Channels of distribution	$ Sales	$ Variable costs*	$ Profit margin	% Sales
A	750,000	400,000	350,000	47
B	250,000	100,000	150,000	60
C	300,000	300,000		
D	200,000	250,000	− 50,000†	− 25†
Total	1,500,000	1,050,000	450,000	30
Less: Nonvariable expense			300,000	
Net profit			150,000	10

B. Estimated Effect of Changes in Channels

Channels of distribution	$ Sales	$ Variable costs*	Net profit
C	− 150,000‡	− 205,000	55,000
D	− 200,000‡	− 250,000	50,000
A and B	100,000§	85,000	15,000
Total	− 250,000	− 370,000	120,000

C. After Changes in Channels

Channels of distribution	$ Sales	$ Variable costs*	$ Profit margin	% Sales
A	825,000	415,000	410,000	50
B	315,000	130,000	185,000	59
C	120,000	110,000	10,000	8
Total	1,260,000	655,000	605,000	48
Less: Nonvariable expense			310,000	
Net profit			295,000	23

* Production plus distribution costs.
† Loss.
‡ Eliminated.
§ Added.

and service. The company investigated the possibility of direct distribution when they saw their wholesaler situation deteriorating rapidly. This deterioration was evidenced by the fact that their other lines, which were distributed direct to industrial users, were increasing in sales at an annual rate of approximately 15 to 20 per cent, while sales of their products through wholesalers were growing at an annual rate of only 6 to 8 per cent. They also knew that total industry sales of this type of product were growing faster. The company's salesmen reported a number of factors which appeared to be responsible for the low rate of increase in sales through wholesale dealers.

Dealers were taking on many additional products, including many competitive products, which were vying for the wholesale salesmen's time. Some dealers were starting to manufacture their own products, competing with the company's products. For all these reasons, dealers were not giving enough attention to the company's line, and sales were suffering.

At the same time, the company's products were becoming more complex technically, and this required more sales engineering before a sale and more service after a sale. Accordingly, a study was made for the company's top management of the consequences and requirements of direct distribution.

Sales Forecast

First, a sales forecast was made of the results of going direct. The regular five-year forecast estimated what sales would be if the company remained with dealers. Then, on the assumption of removal of all the sales-inhibiting factors mentioned above (i.e., dealers' lack of sufficient attention to the company's line) plus better selling by the company's own salesmen, it was forecast how much direct sales would exceed dealer sales. This annual increment in sales as a result of going direct was estimated to be approximately 10 to 12 per cent.

Marketing-cost Forecast

The estimated favorable effect on sales was only the first step in an analysis of the probable results of direct distribution. Next, the company made a realistic projection of the marketing costs of direct distribution, as a basis for forecasting expected net profits. The following kinds of data were gathered and analyzed in the process of estimating direct distribution costs:

1. Data on aggregate dealer sales, dealer inventories, dealer sales and service forces, dealer peculiarities, strengths, and limitations

2. Data on what competitive manufacturers were doing who sold direct; the number of their sales offices and branches with warehouses; the size of their sales and service staffs, and their communications networks

The company also set up certain minimum service requirements. For example, they wanted every customer and every good potential customer to receive a certain number of sales calls per time period. Inventories and warehouses were to be located so that they could deliver by land transportation within twenty-four hours to customers in any industrial center throughout the United States.

Simulation

The above data enabled a simulation to be made of the requirements and costs of direct distribution. The results of this simulation are shown in Table 5.3 (actual figures omitted). The first

Table 5.3   Simulation of effects of direct distribution on marketing costs

Marketing function	No. of units of work	Cost per unit of work	Function costs (2 × 3)
Investment in inventories	Average inventory value	XX	XXX
Warehousing of inventories at branches	Cubic feet of storage space	XX	XXX
Assembling of customer orders	Number of standard handling units	XX	XXX
Credit and collection	Number of customers	XX	XXX
Sales engineering	Number of sales calls	XX	XXX
Service engineering	Number of service calls	XX	XXX
Invoicing, etc.	Number of invoice lines	XX	XXX
Advertising, price lists, catalogues	Number of customers	XX	XXX

column to the left shows the several marketing functions or activities that direct distribution entailed. Some of these would be completely new activities, while others were being performed to some extent even under distribution through dealers. The third column shows a physical measure of the work load estimated for each function. The unit costs in column 3 multiplied by the number of units of work load in the second column yield the total functional costs entered in column 4.

Cost Savings

The above costs were estimated on an annual basis for each of the first four years after a change-over from wholesale distribution to direct marketing. These estimates showed that, in the second or third year after going direct, the company could expect a total distribution-cost ratio (as a percentage of sales) of approximately half that under wholesale-dealer distribution. This "saving" would come about in the following manner:

Wholesalers were given a 30 per cent discount off list prices. In addition, the company had their own staff of sales engineers and servicemen (and carried on advertising to ultimate customers), supplementing and duplicating the dealer's sales and service forces. The costs of these sales and service activities amounted to about 10 to 12 per cent of sales at list prices. Added to the 30 per cent discount, the company's total marketing costs when distributing through wholesalers thus amounted to about 40 per cent of sales at list prices.

It was estimated that wholesale dealers were making about 10 per cent net profit on the company's line. That is, dealer handling costs for the line were probably only about 20 per cent. With direct distribution, the company would "save" this 10 per cent net profit which had been included in the dealers' 30 per cent margin.

Increased Efficiency

Second, the company estimated that it could perform more cheaply and more efficiently some of the functions previously performed by the dealers. For example, the dealers had a cadre of 600 sales engineers. It was estimated that they spent only 10 per cent of their time on the company line (this equaled 60 man-years), and in addition the company had its own sales force backing them up. The same thing was true of servicemen. Thus, it was estimated that combined company and wholesaler man-years of sales and service exceeded that which would be necessary under direct distribution.

With reference to the cost of carrying inventories, it was estimated that the cumulative inventories of the company's line in the hands of all their dealers greatly exceeded the total inventories that would be carried in the company's field warehouses. Finally, it was estimated that the planned marketing and physical distribution plant could readily handle the increased sales volume that was anticipated under direct distribution as a result of better sales and service.

Results

As a result of this analysis, a decision was made to distribute direct. A substantial amount was invested by the company in "starting up" direct distribution. This covered the following elements:

1. Recruiting and training salesmen, sales engineers, and servicemen
2. Setting up field sales offices and warehouses with inventories
3. Setting up a communications network

Two years after the date of announcement of direct distribution, the following results were achieved:

1. Sales increase (over increase budgeted under wholesale distribution), 12 per cent.
2. Marketing costs as per cent of sales declined from 44 to 23 per cent.
3. Net profit as a per cent of sales (on this line) increased from 5 to 18 per cent.

UNPROFITABLE SALES TERRITORIES

Shifting Effort

A marketing-cost analysis in a regional company revealed a marked concentration of profits in a few sales territories. Thus,

territory A earned almost half the company's profits, while territory B brought in a third. Together, these two territories accounted for 82.2 per cent of the total profits. At the other end
of the scale, four territories were shown to be unprofitable.
These were K, J, I, and H, and they were responsible for a loss
which amounted to 6.6 per cent of the firm's marketing profit
contribution. This loss equaled almost $250,000 at an annual
rate (Table 5.4).

Table 5.4   **Profitability analysis
of sales territories**

Territory	% of total $ marketing profit contribution
Total	100.0
A	48.4
B	33.8
C	11.4
D	8.2
E	2.8
F	1.3
G	0.7
Subtotal	106.6
H	−0.6
I	−0.8
J	−1.3
K	−3.9
Subtotal	−6.6

As a result, the following questions were raised for management consideration:

1. Would the total profit contribution be increased if some
marketing efforts were diverted from territories H, I, J, and K to,
say, territory A—or if marketing efforts in the unprofitable territories were simply reduced?

2. Would the profit contribution of the firm be increased if
the unprofitable territories were turned over to wholesalers **for**

handling? (Transportation costs for territory A were only 3.5 per cent of sales, while in K they were 14.8 per cent.)

3. Would the company's profit contribution be increased if unprofitable products X and Y were eliminated only in the unprofitable territories (instead of being eliminated company-wide)?

As a first step, unprofitable products X and Y were discontinued only in unprofitable territories H, I, J, and K. As a result, in the following period, territories H and I reached the break-even point. The rate of loss in the remaining unprofitable territories was considerably reduced. The over-all rate of loss on the unprofitable products X and Y was also reduced substantially.

As a next step, selling and advertising efforts in all four unprofitable territories were reduced, some of the expenditure being shifted to the more profitable territories. The net effect was to make these four territories profitable and to increase the company's profits substantially.

Alternative Territory Expenditures

In one company, the number of salesmen in each area depended largely on the combined sales possibilities of all products in the company's line. But even when this had been determined, by measurement of market potentials, some products were given either more or less selling time by salesmen than their sales possibilities in particular areas appeared to warrant. Salesmen, of course, tend to shift their selling time to the products which sell more easily in their particular territories because of greater opportunities or their own ability and preference. This, in itself, appeared to cause misalignment of selling effort with respect to the regional sales potentials of particular products, thereby affecting the corresponding sales rates.

Furthermore, it was found that the relative importance of different product groups in total sales volume was in itself affected by regional variations in number of salesmen as well as by other conditions. Thus, product group A and especially product group B tended to constitute a smaller proportion of total sales volume in regions where there were very few salesmen; but in areas where more salesmen were employed, their relative

Table 5.5   The effect of varying numbers of salesmen on proportions of product groups A, B, and C in total volume

Salesmen per 1 million persons	Percentages of total volume		
	A	B	C
2	50.0	10.9	37.3
6	50.6	13.9	30.6
10	50.9	14.8	27.5
14	51.1	15.7	25.4
18	51.2	16.3	23.8
22	51.3	16.8	22.7
26	51.4	17.2	21.6
30	51.5	17.6	20.8

sales were greater, and those of C were markedly less (Table 5.5).

Diminishing Returns

These tendencies indicated that diminishing returns from selling effort were greater for some types of products. They also suggested that, for various reasons, the selling of some products required more time and effort. Regional sales managers needed to consider this in deciding whether or not to employ additional salesmen in particular areas or to improve the general performance of the sales force on particular products.

Sales management had also to consider the tendency toward diminishing returns from the selling effort expended on the entire line of products. This tendency is illustrated in Table 5.6, which shows the relationship between the number of units per capita of all products sold and the corresponding number of salesmen working in twelve selling areas selected because of their general similarity. Although larger sales are associated with a greater number of salesmen, the territory with, say, four salesmen will not have four times the sales volume of a territory of equal population having one salesman. Likewise, the sales volume in a four-salesman territory will normally exceed that of a

Table 5.6   Relationship between number of salesmen and volume of sales in twelve country territories

Number of salesmen per 100,000 persons	Annual sales per capita, units	Increase in sales with each additional salesman, units
1	6.4	6.4
2	12.6	6.2
3	17.2	4.6
4	20.8	3.6

three-salesman territory by an amount less than the excess of a three-salesman territory over a two-salesman territory. In short, there is a declining rate of increase in sales as the number of salesmen is increased.

Of course, a measurement in monetary terms of the tendency to diminishing returns enables sales management to see more clearly the most profitable basis of operation and strive for its attainment. The results in monetary terms for the twelve areas described above are shown in Table 5.7.

Since these twelve territories are generally similar except for number of salesmen, the rates of diminishing profits may be approximated by comparing the profits obtained from areas

Table 5.7   Relationship between number of salesmen per territory and profits in twelve country territories

Number of salesmen	Sales volume, units (add 000)	$ Gross margin	$ Sales salary plus variable expense	$ Profit contribution
1	640	6,400	4,086	2,312
2	1,260	11,970	8,142	3,828
3	1,720	16,340	12,096	4,244
4	2,080	18,720	15,952	2,768
Increase with fourth salesman (4–3)	360	2,380	3,856	−1,476*

*Decrease.

with one, two, three, and four salesmen. This would indicate the profits obtained by adding salesmen in one of them. For example, the third salesman, though causing a smaller increase in volume and gross margin than the second, is worth employing, nevertheless, because total profits above variable costs are increased from $3,828 to $4,244. A fourth salesman would increase sales volume by 360,000 units, but a loss of $1,476 would be incurred because the gross profit on this volume, $2,380, is less than enough to cover out-of-pocket expenses of $3,856 (see bottom line of Table 5.7). Clearly, it is not profitable to employ the fourth salesman in this instance.

However, because of regional variations in competition and in population density, occupation, income, and other basic consumption factors, the true diminishing-returns curve for a particular area cannot always be obtained by averaging the results of groups of otherwise similar marketing areas having one, two, three, or more salesmen.

Most Profitable Number of Salesmen

In determining the most profitable number of salesmen and the amount of other efforts to assign to each territory, sales management in this company is also guided by the experience gained through actual marketing experiments in different territories (see Chapter 6). These experiments show the sales, marketing cost, and profit results of changing the number of salesmen or the amounts of other varieties of selling effort in an area.

Other selling efforts, such as advertising and dealer helps, delivery service, and the like, also have their own tendencies toward diminishing returns, which are modified by the number of salesmen and other conditions in each region. In short, many complex and interrelated factors must be considered in determining the most profitable number of salesmen to employ in any marketing territory.

Over a period of years, sales management in this company has been using indexes of sales potentials, marketing-cost analyses, and actual experiments as guides to the most efficient and profitable territorial apportionment of selling effort. Changes in the territorial distribution of selling efforts are constantly being made. Although other influences are of course also responsible, management feels that it is undoubtedly true that these changes are one of the factors (together with customer and product selling policies) responsible for a decline of more than 50 per cent in the ratio of variable marketing expenses to sales over a period of years.

REFERENCE

1. Charles H. Sevin, *How Manufacturers Reduce Their Distribution Costs,* U.S. Department of Commerce, Government Printing Office, Washington, 1948.

chapter six

INCREASING THE PRODUCTIVITY OF ITEMS AND CUSTOMERS BY MARKETING EXPERIMENTS

WHY MARKET EXPERIMENTS ARE NECESSARY

The preceding chapters have shown that marketing-cost analysis frequently suggests changes that will bring about increased productivity, without the need for any further information. But frequently marketing-cost analysis raises a number of questions that remain to be answered before productivity can be increased:

1. By how much (if any) would the net profit contribution of the most profitable products be increased if there were some increase in their marketing expenditures? How would such a change affect the strategy of competitors—would it result in a viable and stable market share?

2. By how much (if any) would the net losses of unprofitable products be reduced if there were some decrease in their total marketing expenditure?

3. By how much (if any) would the profit contributions of profitable products be affected by a change in the marketing expenditures on the unprofitable products, and vice versa? That is, what would be the effects on the entire product line or marketing system?

4. If the marketing mix of the most profitable (and most unprofitable) products were changed, what would be the effects on their net profit contribution? By how much (if any) would their net profit contribution be increased (or decreased) if there were an increase or decrease in advertising?

5. If unprofitable products were eliminated from the line entirely, what would be the effect on profits?

6. By how much (if any) would the total profit contribution be increased if some marketing efforts were to be diverted from unprofitable to profitable territories—or if direct marketing efforts in the unprofitable territories were simply to be reduced?

7. By how much (if any) would the net profit contribution be increased if there were a change in the method of distributing to small unprofitable accounts or if they were eliminated?

There are two implicit assumptions underlying these questions:

1. There is a low or even negative productivity of some marketing efforts absorbed by unprofitable or less profitable segments.

2. There would be a higher productivity of these marketing efforts if they were shifted to the more profitable segments.

If these implicit hypotheses are proved correct, then such shifts in expenditure would obviously result in a substantial over-all increase in productivity.

But how can we predict the effects of shifts in marketing effort from one segment to another or of changes in the marketing mix of any one segment? It is necessary to predict these effects with reasonable accuracy and reliability if the marketing manager is to use this information in making decisions. Furthermore, it is not sufficient to be able to predict the effects of shifts in relatively static terms. It is also necessary to be able to predict the corresponding changes which might be expected to take place in competitors' programs.

It appears that only by the use of actual market experiments is it possible to estimate or predict reliably the effects of changes in marketing expenditures on the sales volume or net profits of each differentiated product, or customer class, or sales territory in a multiproduct, multifunctional business organization. The only way to obtain reliable answers to the preceding questions is on an experimental basis under the real-life conditions of the marketplace [1].

MARKETING EXPERIMENTS WITH PRODUCTS

Elimination of Unprofitable Products

A marketing-cost analysis of a long product line of a certain company revealed that more than two-thirds of the items in the line, 635 out of 875, were exceedingly unprofitable (see Chapter 4). A controlled marketing experiment was run to check:

1. The direct effects on sales and profits of the elimination of most of the unprofitable products (592 out of 635)

2. The indirect effects on the sales and profits of the remainder of the line

Two groups of sales territories were designated by "random" methods of selection; one was a "control" group, and the other was an experimental group. In the experimental group of territories, 592 unprofitable items were eliminated from the line. Total field selling, direct-mail, and other territorial promotional efforts were diverted to the 240 profitable items remaining in the product line. If customers requested any eliminated item, salesmen were instructed to attempt to "switch" them to the nearest substitute.

The experiment was run for eighteen months, in order to allow for any long-run effects of a shortened product line. The experimental results are shown in Table 6.1. Elimination of the unprofitable items apparently had no adverse long-run effects on sales volume. If anything, there appeared to be a small

Table 6.1   Experimental effects of eliminating a large number of unprofitable products from company line

Item	Number of products	% Sales	% Marketing costs	% Net profit contribution
Control territories:				
Profitable products	240	103.5	101.3	114.9
Unprofitable products	635	102.8	103.8	−15.4
Totals or averages (1)	875	103.4	101.5	99.5
Experimental territories:				
Profitable products	240	108.9	111.7	123.8
Unprofitable products	43	102.9	7.0	− .4
Totals or averages (2)	283	108.7	58.2	123.4
Effects of elimination (2–1)	−592	+5.3	−43.3	+23.9

increase in the sale of the profitable items. There would be, however, a substantial increase of around 24 per cent in the company's total profit contribution if the unprofitable products were eliminated. Accordingly, the unprofitable products were eliminated.

Reallocation of Selling Time to Products

Experiments were conducted by another manufacturer for one year in a number of sales territories that involved an increase in salesmen's selling time for profitable product B and a decrease of selling time for unprofitable product L. Table 6.2 shows the experimental results. An increase in product B's selling effort resulted in a substantial increase in its sales volume. A reduction in product L's selling effort resulted in a moderate sales reduction. A substantial increase in profits occurred when the selling effort for product B was increased, while product L's loss was eliminated.

In projecting the experimental results to nationwide company operations, it was forecast that these changes in allocation of selling time would have the following effects:

1. A net increase in total sales volume for products B + L
2. A substantial increase in net profits for products B + L

Table 6.2   Experimental effects of shifting selling time between two
products (in percentages of totals)

Per cent of total selling time			Experi- ment no.	Sales			Profit contribution		
B	L	Total		B	L	Total	B	L	Total
4	17	21	(1)	14.0	12.5	26.5	16.2	−9.0	7.2
10.5	10.5	21	(2)	21.7	9.6	31.3	24.3	−5.4	18.9
17	4	21	(3)	27.2	8.4	35.6	30.8	0.5	31.3
Effect of (2) — (1)				+ 7.7	−2.9	+4.8	+ 8.1	+3.6	11.7
Effect of (3) — (2)				+ 5.5	−1.2	+4.3	+ 6.5	+5.9	12.4
Effect of (3) — (1)				+13.2	−4.1	+9.1	+14.6	+9.5	+24.1

These predictions were used to change national marketing
operations as related to products B and L. In all sales territories, salesmen were instructed to adopt the maximum increase
in selling time for product B and a maximum reduction in selling time for product L.

Elimination of Unprofitable Supermarket Items

As a result of a marketing-cost analysis, a supermarket chain
found that one-third of all items in the dry-grocery and nonfood
departments were unprofitable (see Chapter 4). Ten product
groups were selected for the purpose of running a controlled
experiment to determine the effects of eliminating all unprofitable items from these product groups. The ten groups selected
and their division into profitable and unprofitable items are
shown in Table 6.3.

Ten stores in the chain were selected from one trading area,
divided into two similar groups of five stores each. Two different sets of experiments were run for six weeks each in both
groups of stores; the experimental design is shown in Table 6.4.
In both sets of experiments, all the unprofitable items in the ten
selected product groups were eliminated. This released about
33 per cent of the shelf space previously occupied by these ten
product groups (Table 6.3).

In one set of experiments (experiment 1) the same total

Table 6.3   Dollar net profit contributions, number of items, and space occupied by profitable and unprofitable items in ten product groups in a supermarket (in percentages of totals for ten groups)

Product groups	$ Net profit contribution		Number of items		% Space occupied	
	Profitable items	Unprofitable items	Profitable items	Unprofitable items	Profitable items	Unprofitable items
Ten-group totals	112.6	−12.6	61	39	67	33
Candy, packaged	18.3	− 1.7	10	8	8	3
Cereals, cold	14.1	− 1.4	10	5	6	3
Coffee, regular	12.6	− 1.9	5	3	9	4
Dog food	11.7	− 1.5	5	4	7	3
Detergents, packaged	9.8	− 1.0	6	4	6	5
Coffee, instant	11.2	− 1.1	2	1	6	4
Pickles	8.6	− 0.7	6	2	6	3
Soaps, hand and facial	7.4	− 0.8	6	2	7	2
Flour	7.0	− 0.6	6	2	6	3
Cake mixes	11.9	− 1.9	5	8	6	3

Table 6.4   Experimental design to determine effects of eliminating unprofitable merchandise items in a supermarket

Time period	Group A stores	Group B stores
First 6 weeks	Experiment 1: More space per profitable item; same total space for each experimental product group	Experiment 2: Same space per profitable item; new nonfood items in space made available
Second 6 weeks	Experiment 2: Same space per profitable item; new nonfood items in space made available	Experiment 1: More space per profitable item; same total space for each experimental product group

shelf space that had been occupied by the ten product groups was reserved for them during the experiment. The principal change was the number of shelf facings per remaining profitable item; these were increased to take up the 29 per cent of the space made available. In experiment 2, on the other hand, the number of shelf facings per profitable item during the experiment remained the same as before. The space made available by the elimination of the unprofitable items was allotted to some new nonfood items.

Management Decisions Based on Experimental Results

The results of the experiments are shown in Table 6.5. In both experiments, there was an appreciable increase in dollar gross margins. In experiment 1, where the profitable items were given more selling space, the increase in dollar gross margin amounted to 10.2 per cent. In experiment 2, where new nonfood items occupied the space made vacant by the elimination of the unprofitable items, the dollar gross margin increased by almost 12.5 per cent (Table 6.5).

Table 6.5   Results of an experiment to determine effects of eliminating unprofitable merchandise items in a supermarket

Experiments	$ Average weekly gross margin: 12-week experimental period as % of 12-week period preceding experiments
Experiment 1: Increased space per profitable item; same total space for each experimental product group	110.21
Experiment 2: Same space per profitable item, plus new nonfood items in space made available	112.42
Control stores: Same total space for each experimental product group; same space per item for each profitable and unprofitable item	100.18
Total $ gross margin per store in experimental stores	101.39
Total $ gross margin per store in control stores	100.19

The items eliminated included some small-selling sizes and other minor variations of brands. However, some brands, both controlled and other types, were also eliminated. Yet, total dollar sales and dollar gross margins in the experimental product categories actually increased.*

With higher dollar gross margins and the same lower operating costs, dollar net profits were increased. Because of the favorable results of the experiments, management decided, as a permanent policy, continuously to weed out unprofitable, small-dollar-margin items. Further analysis was made and further experiments were conducted with regard to a few product groups at a time on a rotating basis. It was also decided that a flexible policy should be adopted about the utilization of the shelf space that would be made available in the future.

MARKETING EXPERIMENTS WITH CUSTOMERS

Change in Method of Distributing

A marketing-cost analysis revealed that more than half of all the accounts to whom a national manufacturer distributed direct through company-owned branches and a field sales force were

---

* Management identified the following as the principal factors accounting for the increase in dollar gross margins:

1. In the case of experiment 1, the better display and increased visibility resulting from the substantial increase in number of facings per profitable item probably caused an increase in sales of the profitable items.

2. Because there were fewer items to watch, store clerks found it easier to maintain more nearly fully stocked shelves for the profitable items and a reduction in their out-of-stocks. Increased visibility and availability favorably increased sales.

3. Customers switched to profitable items remaining in stock. Complaints were surprisingly few in number. Customers voluntarily commented on the improved appearance of the stores and stated that it was easier to find items they were looking for. In brief, customer reaction appeared to be favorable.

4. In the case of experiment 2, the dollar sales and gross margin contributed by the new nonfood items were greater than dollar sales and gross margins of the unprofitable items.

Table 6.6   Experimental design to determine effects of changing methods of distributing to unprofitable accounts

	Control	Mail order	Wholesale
Type of customer	Group 1 territories	Group 2 territories	Group 3 territories
Large, profitable customers	Company branches	Company branches	Company branches
Small, unprofitable customers	Company branches	Mail order	Wholesale distributor

substantially unprofitable (see Chapter 5). Market experiments were conducted to test the effects of distributing through wholesalers or on a mail-order basis to these unprofitable accounts.

Three groups of territories were selected, as similar as possible with regard to such factors as urban-rural proportions of the population and economic characteristics of the areas. In these territories, market experiments were conducted according to the scheme of variants shown in Table 6.6. In this way, marketing management obtained quantitative data with regard to the following factors:

1. The dollar sales and gross profits that might be either lost or gained

2. Reductions and additions in variable marketing costs which were likely to result

3. The final effect of the above interrelated factors on the total dollar profit contribution

The results of the experiments at the end of a year are shown in Table 6.7. By subtracting the results in the control group of territories, the net effects of the changes in channels of distribution were obtained. In those territories where the mail-order method was tried, there was a slight loss in sales. This was offset by an increase in sales resulting from more selling time devoted to the profitable accounts. Accordingly, there was a net gain in total sales. The extra expense of the mail-order operation apparently exceeded the eliminated field-selling expense for these small accounts. Thus, the increase in the profit contribution lagged the sales increase.

In those territories where wholesale distribution was employed, there was a small increase in sales to wholesalers as compared with previous direct sales to the small accounts that had been turned over to them. Also, there was a greater increase in sales to the larger accounts that continued to be served by the company branches than in the two other groups of territories. Accordingly, the net increase in sales was 13 per cent.

There was also an 18.1 per cent net increase in dollar profit contribution in the territories where small unprofitable customers

Table 6.7   Results of a market experiment to determine sales and profit response to changes in methods of distributing to unprofitable accounts

	Sales			Net profit contribution
	Profitable accounts	Unprofitable accounts	All accounts	
Group 1 territories (control):	(Company branches)			
Before	100.0	100.0	100.0	100.0
During	104.6	100.7	104.2	102.3
Change	4.6	0.7	4.2	2.3
Group 2 territories:	Company branches	Mail order		
Before	100.0	100.0	100.0	100.0
During	116.7	100.2	115.0	111.8
Change	16.7	0.2	15.0	11.8
Minus: Control change	−4.6	−0.7	−4.2	−2.3
Net change	12.1	−0.5	10.8	9.5
Group 3 territories:	Company branches	Wholesale		
Before	100.0	100.0*	100.0	100.0
During	118.9	102.0	117.2	121.4
Change	18.9	2.0	17.2	21.4
Minus: Control change	−4.6	−0.7	−4.2	−2.3
Net change	14.3	1.3	13.0	18.1

* Previous sales to small accounts when served direct by company.

had been turned over to wholesale distributors. This was in spite of the fact that the occupancy costs of the branches and salesmen's salary costs continued at the same levels as previously. Substantial reductions were achieved, however, in billing, credit and collection, order filling, delivery, and salesmen's travel costs. As a result of these experiments, marketing management adopted a national policy of turning over their small unprofitable accounts to wholesale distributors in those areas where suitable distributors were available.

Reduction in Number of Sales Calls

An intensive statistical analysis in General Electric's Lamp Division clearly demonstrated that all types of customers were being saturated with too many sales calls. This was shown by the fact that there was no difference in the average change in annual sales volume between accounts which received an increased number of sales calls and those which received a decreased number [2]. Many charts such as that of Fig. 6.1 showed that, because accounts were being saturated with sales calls, sales-volume changes represented random fluctuations above and below the plateau, or horizontal line, of the sales-response curves.

As part of the analysis, all accounts were classified according to whether they had an increase or a decrease in number of calls in 1953 as compared with 1952. They were then subclassified according to whether they had an increase or a decrease in 1954. This yielded the four classes of accounts shown in Table 6.7a.

Table 6.7a   Accounts classified by increase or decrease in number of sales calls

	Class of accounts			
	1	2	3	4
1952–1953	+	+	−	−
1953–1954	+	−	+	−

Source: Clark Waid, Donald F. Clark, and Russell L. Ackoff," Allocation of Sales Effort in the Lamp Division of the General Electric Company," *Operations Research*, vol. 4, no. 6, December, 1956, pp. 629ff.

A statistical analysis determined whether or not there was any significant change in average dollar sales volume between classes 1 and 2 and classes 3 and 4. No significant changes were found. The sales volume of accounts that received an increase or a decrease in sales calls in one year was unaffected on the average by whether or not they received an increase or a decrease in sales calls in the succeeding years.

These and other, similar analyses clearly suggested to management that "some" reduction in number of sales calls could have been made without reducing sales volume at all. But how much of a decrease in sales calls (average time per sales call did not vary significantly) could have been made without reducing the sales made to these accounts? The available data supported the hypothesis that the accounts were saturated with sales calls, but they did not indicate the extent or the effects on profits of that saturation.

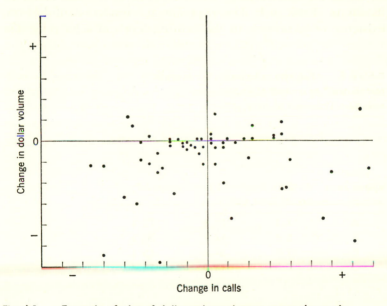

Fig. 6.1   Example of plot of dollar-volume change versus change in number of sales calls. (*Clark Waid, Donald F. Clark, and Russell L. Ackoff, "Allocation of Sales Effort in the Lamp Division of the General Electric Company,"* Operations Research, *vol. 4, no. 6, December, 1956, pp. 629ff.*)

Another manufacturer (*not* General Electric) made a similar series of statistical analyses. This company also found that accounts were so saturated with sales calls that there was no significant relationship between increases and decreases in number of sales calls and increases and decreases in sales per customer. Furthermore, a marketing-cost and profitability analysis revealed important differences between different types of accounts in their dollar profit contribution per sales call—a large number of accounts being unprofitable.

Accordingly, market experiments were conducted in four groups of territories (one being the "control" group), extending for a period of eighteen months. The profit and sales responses to a 20 per cent, a 33⅓ per cent, and a 50 per cent reduction in the number of sales calls on various classes of accounts were determined in the other three groups of territories.

The average net changes in these groups of test areas, after adjusting for (subtracting) the changes in the control areas, are shown in Table 6.8. The experiments clearly established the existence of saturation in the existing levels of sales calls. The

Table 6.8   Percentage increases in net profit contribution* as a result of experimental reductions in number of sales calls

Account volume class	Percentage reduction in number of sales calls		
	20	33	50
A	11.3	18.6	12.4
B	8.6	14.7	20.2
C	12.9	21.4	15.1
D	7.5	16.8	29.4
.	.	.	.
.	.	.	.
.	.	.	.
N	6.8	18.7	8.9

* After adjusting for (subtracting) changes in control areas.

profit response curves (to number of sales calls) varied between different classes of accounts but apparently approached their maxima somewhere in the area of 66 and 50 per cent (or less) of the base levels of sales calls.

On the basis of these experimental results, marketing management set new company-wide standards of number of sales calls by type of account—generally involving reductions of between $33\frac{1}{3}$ and 50 per cent. At the end of the first year, there were no significant changes in total company (increased) sales trends. There was, however, a large reduction in the total size of the sales force (many of the men were shifted to a new product line introduced by a separate division of the company as part of the over-all planned change). Finally, even in the first year, there was a better than 20 per cent increase in the division's net profit contribution. This increase was clearly attributable to the reduction in the number of sales calls, permitting a reduction in the size of the sales force.

Changed Allocation of Selling Time

A company supplying a large metropolitan area with a service conducted controlled market experiments to determine whether or not the productivity of personal selling could be improved by a different allocation of selling time to various sized groups of customers and prospects [3]. About one-third of the time devoted to sales calls was spent with regular customers or prospects known to be worthwhile, one-third was spent in door-to-door canvasses to locate new prospects, and one-third was spent with customers of either unknown or unimportant size who had invited bids for specific jobs.

A market survey made it possible to determine the size and distribution of the total potential market for its service in the area covered by the company. To management the most striking result of the survey was the distribution of the potential according to customer size. Thus, out of 13,000 potential customers, only 520, or 4 per cent of the total number, accounted for one-half the total annual industry revenue from the service concerned. A second result of the market survey was the discovery that over 88 per cent of the potential customers concentrated their purchasing of this service. That is, each favored some single source of supply to the extent of giving him over half its business.

The findings of the survey suggested to management some immediate changes in directing salesmen's use of their time, on which subsequent experimentation was concentrated. Much of the previous solicitation time had been aimed at getting individual jobs and searching for new prospects. The survey results suggested that the main goal of solicitation should be to become the favored source of supply of the company's relatively small number of large customers and the relatively small number of known large potential customers.

Each of 18 of the company's 35 salesmen was assigned 36 customers for the experiment, so that a total of about 550 customers were involved. The customers in the low-level group were to receive only one hour of sales effort per month; those in the medium-level group, four hours; and those in the high-level group were to receive sixteen hours of sales effort per month. The previous average level was two hours per month per customer.   The experiment was run for four months.

The reaction of the customer to the experiment was measured as follows: For each customer in the experiment, the market survey established his potential, i.e., the total amount currently spent by the customer on this service, either with this company or with its competitors. A customer was considered to have "responded" to the experiment if the company's share of his total potential increased by a "significant" number of percentage points. The actual sales effort expanded during the experiment was often not what had been planned. However, it usually differed considerably from the previous rate. The percentages of customers in each effort group who responded, i.e., who tended to view the company as their favorite supplier by concentrating a larger fraction of their business with the company, is shown in the tabulation.

Rate of selling effort	% Customers responding
Under 7 hours per month	8
7–11 hours per month	53
Over 11 hours per month	40

A statistical analysis was then made to determine whether or not the responses observed could have resulted from chance increases not directly related to increased sales effort. The conclusion from this statistical analysis was that the sequence of responses could not be explained by chance; rather, they implied deliberate, continuing business from the customers. This was substantiated by the opinions of the salesmen involved in the experiment.

The experiment showed that the seven- to eleven-hour rate was the most effective. Under seven hours would seem to be too small to be noticed. Over eleven hours of selling effort showed sharply diminishing returns because a saturation effect may have set in; this amount of time is apparently more than the customer wants. The experiment further indicated strongly that the most profitable subjects for longer sales calls were customers with the largest potential. The larger potential customers were somewhat less likely to respond, i.e., to switch their favorite source of supply. However, the size of the response, when it did occur, more than made up for the difficulty in obtaining the response. In a typical group, experimental selling hours spent on the customers above medium size were $2\frac{1}{2}$ times as productive as hours spent on the customers below medium size, in terms of sales increase per unit of sales effort.

With its new allocation of selling effort based on the results of these experiments, the company's sales force of thirty-five men increased total sales volume by $33\frac{1}{3}$ per cent, from 6 million dollars a year to about 8 million

REFERENCES

1. Richard E. Quandt, "Estimating Advertising Effectiveness: Some Pitfalls in Econometric Models," *Journal of Marketing Research*, vol. 1, no. 2, May, 1964, p. 51.
2. Clark Waid, Donald F. Clark, and Russell L. Ackoff, "Allocation of Sales Effort in the Lamp Division of the General Electric Company," *Operations Research*, vol. 4, no. 6, December, 1956, pp. 629ff.
3. Arthur A. Brown, Frank T. Hulswit, and John D. Kettelle, "A Study of Sales Operations," *Operations Research*, vol. 4, no. 3, June, 1956, pp. 296ff.

chapter seven

INCREASING THE PRODUCTIVITY OF ADVERTISING BY MARKETING EXPERIMENTS

Marketing-cost analysis alone may indicate courses of action that bring about increased productivity. It may also have to be followed by marketing experiments to provide all the information necessary to achieve increased productivity. In this chapter, we discuss one important element of the marketing mix, i.e., advertising, where marketing experiments alone, without prior marketing-cost analysis, may provide a sufficient information base to facilitate productivity increases.

In this chapter, we are primarily concerned with the use of marketing experiments to determine the answer to the following question: By how much (if any) would the sales and net profit contribution of a specific product (whether profitable or unprofitable) be increased or decreased if there were an increase or decrease in its advertising?

REDUCTION OF ADVERTISING ON MATURE PRODUCT

There were numerous reasons for believing that the level of advertising expenditures on a particular mature product in one company were "too high." It was hypothesized that, even though sales volume might suffer somewhat, the product's long-run cumulative profit contribution for the remainder of its life cycle would be appreciably increased if advertising expenditure for it were reduced. Market experiments were used to test this hypothesis.

A series of marketing experiments in a selected number of territories were used to determine the effects of both increases and decreases in spot TV and newspaper advertising on the sales and profits of this particular product. The experiments were conducted long enough and so designed as to be able to estimate the "carry-over," or long-range effects, of changes in the levels of advertising efforts.

Effects of Varying Levels

The scheme of variation is illustrated in the box at the top of Fig. 7.1. The base, or standard, level of advertising is labeled (1) in the center of the box, and the four variants are labeled (2), (3), (4), and (5) in the corners of the box. In this experiment, the base levels of expenditure were doubled and halved. Sales and profit responses from the experiments are shown in the table below the box in Fig. 7.1.

First the average responses, i.e., the average responses in all experimental territories of each of the five variants, are shown, arranged in the same order as in the box above. Below this are shown the "effects" of the variants, i.e., of each level of advertising effort on the sales-and-profit response. These effects are each calculated simply as the differences in the average values of the responses at the two levels of the advertising-effort variables.*

A doubling of advertising had only a negligible effect (if any) on increasing sales, while it clearly had a substantial effect in reducing net profit. A reduction in advertising expenditures, on the other hand, resulted in a relatively small decrease in

* The values referred to above and shown in Fig. 7.1 are calculated

sales volume but in a substantial increase in net profits. In other words, the reduction in advertising expenditures greatly exceeded lower gross margins resulting from lower sales volume.* Accordingly, marketing management adopted the experimental results as the new "standard" marketing operation on a national basis. Television and newspaper advertising expenditures were reduced in all territories for this particular product.

RELATIVE EFFECTIVENESS OF MEDIA

Marketing experiments conducted by the Ford Motor Company on four different advertising media, newspapers, radio, TV, and outdoor advertising, were described as follows [1]:

> It is possible to design experiments in which the advertising is run in a randomly selected group of test areas while in a group of

---

as follows:

Effect	Value
TV, sales and profits	$(3 + 4) - (2 + 5) \div 2$
Newspaper, sales and profits	$(3 + 5) - (2 + 4) \div 2$
Interaction	$(2 + 3) - (4 + 5) \div 2$
Change in mean	$(2 + 3 + 4 + 5) - (4 \times 1) \div 5$

The effect referred to in Fig. 7.1 as the "change in mean" is simply the grand average for all the variants minus the average for the standard, or base, condition. It is therefore an estimate of the difference in average sales-and-profit response in the territories where the experiments are run, resulting from the use of the experimental levels of advertising. The change in mean thus supplies a continuous measure of the "cost" of obtaining information by marketing experiments (in terms of any lost sales or profits). These costs, of course, refer only to the territories where the experiments were being run. Usually, such experimental costs are negligible and are redeemed many times over by the value of the permanent improvements in marketing operations.

* For the purpose of this decision, gross margins were calculated on the basis of sales revenues minus direct manufacturing labor and materials. Thus, by excluding manufacturing overhead, the gross margins used were *higher* than in the accounting records.

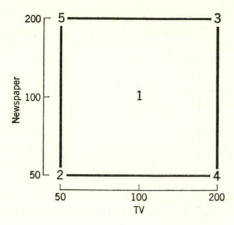

	Sales		Profit contribution	
Average experimental results	32.6	33.9	67.6	60.2
		32.8		71.3
	32.3	33.4	76.2	73.2
95% error limits		±0.7		±1.1
Effects with 95% error limits TV		1.2 ± 0.7		−5.2 ± 1.1
Newspaper		0.4 ± 0.7		−10.8 ± 1.1
Interaction		0.1 ± 0.7		−2.2 ± 1.1
Change in mean		0.2 ± 0.6		−1.6 ± 1.0
Standard deviation		1.44		2.12
95% error limits	1.22	1.76	1.00	2.59

Fig 7.1   Market experiment to determine effects of TV and newspaper advertising on a product's sales and profits.

No newspapers				Newspapers			
No radio		Radio		No radio		Radio	
No TV	TV	No TV	TV	No TV	TV	No TV	TV
No outdoor							
1	2	3	4	5	6	7	8
Outdoor							
9	10	11	12	13	14	15	16

Fig. 7.2   Sixteen-area multimedia experimental design. (*George H. Brown, "Measuring the Sales Effectiveness of Alternative Media,"* Proceedings, Seventh Annual Conference, Advertising Research Foundation, New York, 1961.)

control areas the advertising is not run. This technique can be applied to newspapers and to a growing number of magazines. It is also currently necessary to apply a similar technique to the broadcast media such as TV, radio, and outdoor advertising. However, it is possible to develop and execute experimental designs for each of the major media.

In fact, it is now realistic to consider more sophisticated experimental designs in which several media are tested simultaneously. Such a design not only makes possible the measurement of the sales effectiveness of each medium included in the design, but creates the opportunity to determine the "interaction" between two media or the possibility that because one medium supports another medium the two in combination are more successful than the same amount of money spent on either one of the media separately. Finally, such a design also gives a first approximation to the question of how much money can be spent on advertising since several levels of expenditure are contained in the design. The chart [Fig. 7.2] shows an example of a four-medium experiment involving 16 sets of geographic areas. . . .

The Ford Motor Company has been directing some of its advertising research along the lines outlined. . . . Characteristically, the duration of the test period is a full model year with a six-month "before" period and an eighteen-month "after" period. Allowing for the lag in obtaining and processing the data, a period of three calendar years may be involved in a single test. . . . I can say that our research to date has revealed (1) a demonstrable relationship between advertising and sales, and (2) no significant superiority or infirmity for any one of the limited number of media for which we have completed enough tests to warrant drawing conclusions.

The same writer has cautioned that, because of copy differences and other factors, conclusions from marketing experiments as to the relative sales effectiveness of alternative media should be drawn with care [1]:

> With such experiments as have been described, it is possible to determine the relative sales effectiveness of alternative media under a particular set of copy approaches, presumably the set of copy approaches that is being used in the advertising of the product. However, it is possible that some other combination of copy approaches would not only achieve greater sales results for each of the media but the relative productivity of the media would change. As long as the possibility of such a situation exists, the relative sales effectiveness of alternative media cannot be measured in a single test. Because it is not possible to use a medium without a copy approach of some sort, in theory it is not possible to determine the relative effectiveness of alternative media regardless of the number of tests using different copy approaches. In view of the infinite number of creative ideas, there still might exist some copy approach that would have a major impact on media effectiveness. However, for all practical purposes a series of three or four tests would serve to make significant progress towards the measurement of relative sales effectiveness of alternative media for a specific product.

SALES EFFECTIVENESS OF VARYING LEVELS OF ADVERTISING

A large integrated oil company performed a market experiment in order to determine how much it should spend on advertising [2]. These experiments had the following features:

1. The experiments were run for three years, in order to give sufficient time for the advertising changes to take effect and for various "uncontrolled" factors, such as competitive effort, economic effects, and management changes, to even themselves out.

2. A large number of cities were divided into four groups of test areas, which received the following levels of advertising:

   a. Control group

    b. Half of base-period advertising budget

    c. Double amount of advertising, "double-power"

    d. Triple amount of advertising, "triple-power"

    3. Advertising was increased in test areas at the same annual increment as the rest of the company. The advertising agency selected copy and media, as before, and they were kept constant throughout the whole market area.

    4. Sales results were measured in terms of gallons sold in company-owned service stations in the four groups of markets.

    5. Markets were chosen for the test on the basis of geographic dispersion and demographic characteristics in areas where the company had a fairly high per cent of distribution and where economic conditions were judged to be of a stable nature.

    The results of the market tests, after making adjustments for previous sales trends in each of the market groups, are shown in Table 7.1. Management analyzed these experimental results as follows [2]:

> *Double-power* market average gallonages increased 16.9% during the first year of double advertising when compared to the estimated trend line [for the first year]. During the second year of double advertising, the average gallonage increased 22.6% compared with the trend and during the third year displayed an increase of 36.2% compared with the trend. The *triple-power* market averages increased [only] 15.5%, 11.2%, and 16.3%, compared with the triple-power trend line [for the first, second, and third years respectively].

Table 7.1   Results of market experiment using various-sized advertising budgets (net percentage increases in gallonage from 1950–1955 trends)

	% Increases in gallonage		
Advertising budget	1956	1957	1958
Double advertising	16.9	22.6	36.2
Triple advertising	15.5	11.2	16.3

Source: "Missouri Valley Petroleum Company," case study of the Harvard University Graduate School of Business Administration, Boston, Mass., 1963. Reproduced by permission of the President and Fellows of Harvard College.

Briefly then, in three years of testing advertising effectiveness, the double-power markets had shown sales increases twice as great as those shown by the triple-power markets. Thus, company officials expected, within certain limits, that a doubling of advertising would actually foster a greater sales increase than would a triple advertising schedule.

As for the *half-power* market, . . . apparently the reduced advertising had neither a favorable nor unfavorable effect on sales when compared with the control group. . . . Advertising was reinstated in the half-power cities with no appreciable impact during that year on the sales trend.

A test marketing and advertising experiment was designed by Du Pont to determine whether or not the market for Teflon* (nonstick cookware) could be revived by means of an improved product and a television consumer advertising program [3]. If so, Du Pont also wanted to know what level of advertising would be necessary to move Teflon cookware in significant quantities.

The experimental design that was used is shown in Table 7.2. This design permitted the testing of three levels of adver-

* Teflon, TFE-fluorocarbon resin finish.

Table 7.2   Experimental design for testing effects on sales of television advertising

| | Fall | | |
Following winter	High advertising: 10 daytime advertisements per week	Low advertising: 5 daytime advertisements per week	No advertising
High advertising: 10 daytime advertisements per week	Detroit Springfield	Dayton	Wichita
Low advertising: 5 daytime advertisements per week	Columbus	St. Louis Bangor Youngstown	Rochester
No advertising	Omaha	Pittsburgh	Philadelphia Grand Rapids

Source: Malcolm A. McNiven, "Measuring the Effectiveness of Industrial Advertising," *Proceedings, Ninth Annual Conference, Advertising Research Foundation*, New York, 1963.

tising under controlled conditions at the same time. In addition, the design would show the combined effect of all sequences of advertising levels.

Sales were measured during each test period by telephone interviews with random samples of 1,000 female heads of households in each test market. These sales measurements showed that markets with a low level of advertising did no better than the markets with no advertising level. Accordingly, in the subsequent analyses, the no-advertising and the low-advertising markets were combined to give a more substantial basis for the averages.

The results of the experiments are shown in Table 7.3. Purchases of Teflon-coated cookware in the group of markets exposed to a high level of advertising during both the fall and winter test periods were almost three times purchases in markets where little or no advertising was done during both test periods (seventy versus twenty-five).

The experimental results also showed that the effect of high winter advertising alone on winter sales was more than twice as great as the effect of high fall advertising alone on fall sales. Finally, the experimental data indicate that there was a definite positive carry-over effect on the following winter's sales from the preceding fall advertising at the high advertising level.

Du Pont concluded from the experimental results that the market for cookware coated with Teflon was indeed brought to

Table 7.3   Experimental effects on sales of television advertising. Purchases of cookware units coated with Teflon per 1,000 female heads of households, in winter period

Following winter	Fall	
	Low TV advertising	High TV advertising
Low TV advertising	25	32
High TV advertising	49	70

Source: Malcolm A. McNiven, "Measuring the Effectiveness of Industrial Advertising," *Proceedings, Ninth Annual Conference, Advertising Research Foundation,* New York, 1963.

life with an improved product and a certain high level of advertising. (The experimental results also would enable Du Pont to estimate whether the additional Teflon sales compared with the additional advertising costs would result in a worthwhile addition to net profits.)

Du Pont further concluded from the test marketing and advertising experiment that ". . . it is possible for an advertiser to measure the effects of his advertising on the sales of his or his customer's products. It is no longer necessary to sit and bemoan the fact that we can never measure the effects of advertising on sales of our products. The experimental techniques described here are practical, feasible, and accurate [3]."

EFFECTS OF ADVERTISING ON TERRITORIAL PROFITABILITY

In order to measure the territorial effects of advertising on sales and profits, Du Pont conducted a series of market experiments on a product with the following characteristics [4]:

1. The product was a consumer product and was associated by consumers with Du Pont. . . .
2. The product was distributed nationally, which would permit variation in advertising expenditures in several areas.
3. The product was sold during a relatively short season. This would simplify problems of measuring advertising results, since less attention would have to be paid to "carryover" effects during an extended period of time.
4. The product was "mature" and relatively stable. The same major competing brands had been sold in essentially the same manner for many years, and there had been no major innovations or changes in marketing practices. Relatively good information on sales, market shares, market potential, etc., was available for the product.

To secure meaningful measures of sales response to advertising, substantial increases in advertising expenditures were made in the test areas. Three different advertising "treatments" were used, the same level of expenditure as in the base period, $2\frac{1}{2}$ times normal, and 4 times normal, at each of three Du Pont market-share levels. (The preliminary investigation suggested that a major factor affecting response to advertising was the existing market share of the Du Pont brand.)

The advertising in each area included some national media (network TV) and local media such as newspapers. In areas selected to receive above-normal expenditures, the additional advertisements were placed in local media. Consequently, the advertising treatments unavoidably differed in the distribution of expenditures among media as well as in total dollars.

On the basis of the experimental results and other data, it was possible to estimate the profit contribution resulting from a given advertising expenditure in a given territory. This profit contribution or marginal profit was defined as sales dollars minus variable cost.

Before the experiments, the profitability of advertising in all trading areas in all of Du Pont's fifty-six sales territories for this product was determined. The results showed a variation in profit contribution per dollar of advertising of $2\frac{1}{2}$ to 1 as between the highest and lowest areas. Accordingly, parts of the advertising budget were experimentally reallocated from some of the least profitable territories to the most profitable ones.

A second series of market experiments and related analyses were conducted in the following year, which substantiated predictions based on the previous year's experiments. As a result of the two-year study, one of the principal recommendations to Du Pont management was the following [4]:

> Because the variability among trading areas in profit return per additional advertising dollar is so large, it is recommended that the allocation of future [advertising] budgets [to trading areas] use the method developed in this project as a guide, so as to generate either more sales from the same budget, or the same sales with a lower budget.

SEGMENTATION OF CONSUMER MARKETS

A manufacturer determined after extensive market research that significant segments of the ultimate consumer market for one of his products were:

1. Various income levels of the male head of the family
2. The different "purposes" that consumers had in mind when they purchased the product

Further market research revealed, for both these types of market segments:

1. Per cent of total industry sales of this product (i.e., sales of all brands combined)
2. Per cent of total sales to "brand switchers" (i.e., sales to consumers who changed from one brand to another)

This information was summarized as shown in Table 7.4.

The company had allocated advertising effort to consumer segments according to the criterion of per cent of total industry sales (i.e., the top figure in each cell shown in Table 7.4). It

Table 7.4 Percentages of total and brand-switcher sales by income and purpose-of-purchase consumer-market segments

| Income of male head of household and percentage of sales | Purpose of purchase | | | |
	Purpose A	Purpose B	Purpose C	Total
Under $6,000:				
% of total industry sales	4	5	4	13
% of total brand-switcher sales	3	4	3	10
$6,000 to $12,000:				
% of total industry sales	11	10	19	40
% of total brand-switcher sales	18	17	9	44
$12,000 to $18,000:				
% of total industry sales	8	9	16	33
% of total brand-switcher sales	18	14	6	38
Over $18,000:				
% of total industry sales	1	5	8	14
% of total brand-switcher sales	*	4	4	8
Total:				
% of total industry sales	24	29	47	100
% of total brand-switcher sales	39	39	22	100

* Less than 1 per cent.

was proposed to marketing management that, instead, the short-term objective of advertising effort should be to capture as many as possible of the brand switchers that exist at any point in time (i.e., according to the bottom figures in each cell). It was demonstrated (mathematically) that in this way the company could most rapidly increase its share of the total market.

A markedly different allocation of advertising effort was indicated by the objective of capturing brand switchers. In order to determine the effects of the proposed change in the allocation of effort, a controlled marketing experiment was made.

The experiment was conducted in several territories. A substantial shift was made in the percentages of the advertising budget aimed at appealing to consumers who had different purposes in mind in purchasing the product. Thus, for example, the per cent of the advertising budget directed toward purpose C was reduced from 50 per cent of the total to only 15 per cent, while the budgets for purposes A and B were increased from 25 to 45 and 40 per cent, respectively.

In order to implement these experimental changes in the advertising budget, both different copy appeals and changes in media mix were required. The changed media mix actually involved a net reduction in the dollar advertising budget of more than 10 per cent.

These experimental changes succeeded in capturing a larger percentage of the brand switchers. Increases in sales volume were more than 12 per cent. Accordingly, there was an 18 per cent increase in the total dollar net profit contribution of this product in the experimental territories. Consequently, this change in the allocation of the advertising budget was adopted on a company-wide basis.

REFERENCES

1. George H. Brown, "Measuring the Sales Effectiveness of Alternative Media," *Proceedings, Seventh Annual Conference, Advertising Research Foundation,* New York, 1961.
2. "Missouri Valley Petroleum Company," case study of the Harvard

University Graduate School of Business Administration, Boston, Mass., 1963. Reproduced by permission of the President and Fellows of Harvard College.

3. Malcolm A. McNiven, "Measuring the Effectiveness of Industrial Advertising," *Proceedings, Ninth Annual Conference, Advertising Research Foundation,* New York, 1963.
4. "Measurement of the Effects of Advertising," E. I. du Pont de Nemours & Company, case study of the Harvard University Graduate School of Business Administration, Boston, Mass., 1963. Reproduced by permission of the President and Fellows of Harvard College.

chapter eight

MARKETING-EXPERIMENT INFORMATION

SOME PROBLEMS IN CONDUCTING MARKETING EXPERIMENTS

It is widely believed that experimentation in marketing, as described in the two preceding chapters, is not a feasible method for obtaining information on which important decisions can be based. Market experiments are very difficult to plan and execute and consume considerable amounts of time and money. It cannot even be guaranteed in advance that the results of the experiments will be statistically significant and useful. Sales executives are also often reluctant to undertake marketing experiments because they are fearful that even temporary and limited experimental changes will unfavorably affect sales and customer relationships, perhaps for some period into the future as well as during the course of the experiments.

Experimental procedure is typically (but erroneously) thought of as a situation in which the experimenter needs to "control," i.e., "hold constant" all variables or factors affecting the marketing system except one variable, such as advertising, for example, whose effect or response is being determined. But the real-world marketplace is exceedingly complex. There are a large number of variables which affect the sales and profit responses that are beyond the marketing man's control. There are also many important forces or states of nature affecting the sales and profit response of a particular product which are not even known.

Other important problems involved in marketing experimentation have been outlined [1] as follows:

1. Market experiments frequently are used for measuring short-term response, but long-term response is often more relevant. The problem of carry-over effects (from one time period to the next) may be serious. Many marketing innovations require changes in buyer habits and may "catch on" only after marketing effort has been exerted over a considerable period of time. An experiment that accurately measures short-term response may reduce so small a part of the uncertainty surrounding a decision as to be of limited usefulness.

2. It is usually expensive to measure accurately the actual sales response in individual experimental units. If small geographic areas such as sales territories or metropolitan areas are used, accurate sales figures often can be obtained only at substantial added expense. Whether sales to retailers or to the ultimate consumer are to be used, it is obvious that the manufacturer's accounting records of deliveries to wholesalers (which are the usual record of the manufacturer's sales) are inadequate. Changes in wholesalers' inventories and trading by wholesalers across the boundaries of the manufacturer's sales territories render accounting records inadequate. (Sometimes the sales records of wholesalers, if they will cooperate, are helpful.) When retail stores are the experimental unit, special retail-store audits or successive shelf counts may be needed. In short, the expense of securing accurate sales measurements is often large.

3. Variability of sales between experimental units that receive identical experimental treatments is often large by comparison with the responses to marketing action that are being

measured by the experiments. Even the most ingenious experimental design may sometimes not suffice to reduce uncontrolled variation in sales to the point where the response can be accurately measured unless an economically exorbitant experiment size is used.

4. It is difficult to prevent "contamination" of control units by test units. Few marketing expenditures can really be directed only to specific experimental units, such as individual territories. Local advertising media spread out widely from their area of primary focus, wholesalers and retailers have overlapping trading areas, and recipients of mail-order catalogues talk with each other. All these illustrations are examples of contamination. The experimental stimuli not only reach the test units but via the test units reach some of the control units as well, thus making the test-control comparison impure and somewhat obscure.

5. It is often difficult to make marketing experiments sufficiently realistic to be useful. National advertising media usually (but not always) have to be used "as is" and thus often cannot be adapted to experiments; and usually they cannot be experimented with per se as can local media. Another serious problem in attaining realism stems from the fact that competitors may not respond or react to local experimental actions but then will react later to these actions if adopted as a general policy. At the other extreme, competition may be unusually energetic in "jamming" the experiment once competitors learn of it.

SOME FEASIBLE APPROACHES TO MARKETING EXPERIMENTS

While all the above-outlined problems are often discouraging, they do not rule out experimentation as a feasible and fruitful information base for increasing the productivity of marketing operations. Experimental methods have been developed and used with extremely productive results in such diverse fields as agriculture, biology, and continuous-process manufacturing. In these fields it is also impossible to know, let alone control, all the relevant variables. The experimental methods developed in these diverse fields fit well the complex situations in marketing. For example, compare the situation in agricultural experiments [2]:

> The agricultural experimenter who wants to know which of a thousand factors makes a certain plant grow better faces a situation similar to the marketing man who wants to increase his sales. As a rule, neither of them can know, let alone control, all the factors that affect his situation. The agricultural experimenter realizes that it is impossible to have every seed planted in soil of exactly the same composition; the sun, the wind, the rain, insects, all of nature is notoriously indifferent to man's wishes. Yet a great deal of extremely productive [experimental] research has been carried out under these conditions.

The reason why experimental methods can be successfully used in marketing is simply that, in broad terms, the objective is a comparison of alternative treatments, for example, to determine which of two or more alternatives is "better" for increasing sales or profits. Unlike "scientific" experiments whose objective may be to "discover" an absolute quantity like the speed of light, marketing experiments do not try to measure a single absolute value precisely.

Since it is not the objective in marketing experiments to arrive at absolute values, experimental techniques do *not* require recognition or even control of all the variables that are involved. All that is necessary is to compare the responses of several alternatives in such a way that nothing in the experimental procedure itself will favor, or "bias," one or more of the alternatives over the others.

Another way of putting this is that the actual level of the sales or profit response is, of course, affected by all the uncontrolled and unrecognized variables or factors present in the various sales territories or time periods (or other experimental units) used in the experiment. But the differences in sales between the various alternatives under investigation should not be affected by these uncontrolled and unrecognized factors. With a good experimental design, all alternatives are exposed equally to the same set of uncontrolled and unrecognized variables.

EXPERIMENTAL RESPONSE-SURFACE EXPLORATIONS

In conducting market experiments, the objective is the exploration of how sales and net profits respond to changes in a number
of marketing-effort variables or factors. The mathematician or
statistician would say that the experimenter is concerned with
elucidating certain aspects of a functional relationship, expressed
mathematically as follows:

$$N = \phi\,(X_1, X_2, \ldots, X_k;\; Q_1, Q_2, Q_3, \ldots, Q_p)$$

Connecting a response N, such as sales or net profits, with
the levels $X_1, X_2, \ldots, X_k$ of a group of controlled variables or
factors like magazine advertising, newspaper advertising, radio
and TV advertising, personal selling, sales promotion, etc., k in
number, where $Q_1, \ldots, Q_p$ are unknown parameters [3, 4].

Geometric Representation

The functional relationship between the sales, or net profit
response, and the variable levels, i.e., the marketing-expenditure
levels, can be visualized geometrically by a "response surface."
A useful geometric representation of the response surface is

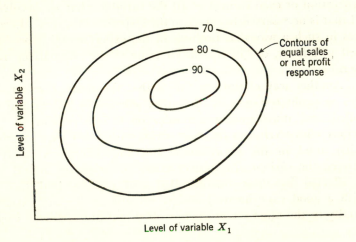

Fig. 8.1   Contours of a two-factor response surface.

obtained by drawing lines of equal sales, or net profit response, on a graph whose coordinates denote the levels of the marketing-effort factors. This type of representation is commonly used in ordinary maps to show the rise and fall of land and in weather charts to show the distribution of equal atmospheric pressure or temperature (see Fig. 8.1).

Market Experiments and Response Surfaces

The marketing executive probably will not become omniscient so that he will know the complete and correct response surface for each important product in his line. This is because a very extensive series of marketing experiments is necessary to determine a complicated response surface with sufficient precision for reliable conclusions to be drawn. Such an extensive series of experiments would, under present conditions, usually be uneconomical and unfeasible.

However, even portions of response surfaces which related sales, or net profit response, to a few different levels of only two or three selected types of marketing expenditures for each important product would be invaluable to the marketing executive. Such limited but most valuable information can be obtained from a relatively small number of experiments.

Moreover, the very concept of a response surface itself is of the greatest value. By suggesting the form of the underlying marketing-effort (marketing-mix) combinations that are of most significance for the marketing system of each product, the concept of the response surface provides indispensable guidance in performing market experiments most efficiently with the object of improving productivity.

When the forms of the "true" response surface and the "true" functional relationship are unknown, the object of market experiments is to approximate them within a given limited experimental region. By means of a series of market experiments, carried out for two or three variables at a time, and covering a relatively wide range in variable levels, approximation to the actual response surface can be roughly plotted. The experiments would center around or be located near the present method of marketing operation. The problem, stated geometrically, is to find the point or points of "maximum" sales, or profit response, in or near this experimental region of the marketing-effort levels.

Method of Steepest Ascent

To find this maximum sales, or net profit response, in a limited experimental region, a series of market experiments are, in effect, used to explore a portion of the response surface by means of "hill climbing," or "steepest ascent." The market experiments may proceed sequentially, i.e., iteratively. The results of one set of experiments may be used to decide the location of the next set of experiments [5].

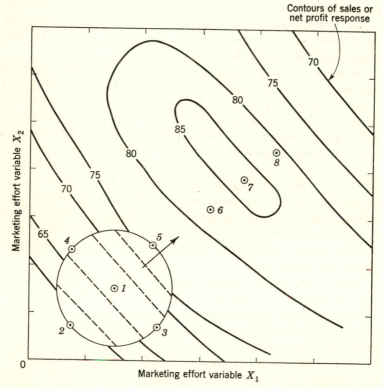

Fig. 8.2   Contour representation of a response surface and first-order experimental design. (*Adapted from G. E. P. Box, "The Exploration and Exploitation of Response Surfaces: Some General Considerations and Examples," Biometrics, vol. 10, no. 1, 1954.*)

Suppose in Fig. 8.2 that the best-known conditions are at the point labeled 1. A suitable experimental design then consists of the origin point 1, together with the four further points 2, 3, 4, and 5. The response contours resulting from this experiment might have the appearance shown by the dashed lines in Fig. 8.2. These fitted contours differ somewhat from the contours of the true (but unknown) response surface. This difference is due, first, to the inability of the simple experimental approximation to represent accurately the "real" response surface and, second, to experimental error. In the example illustrated, however, the representation is obviously quite adequate to allow progress to be made in improving productivity.

To proceed to a region where the sales-and-profit response is even greater, it is natural to follow the direction indicated (in Fig. 8.2) by the arrow at right angles to the contours of the fitted surface resulting from the first series of experiments. Experiment 6 would indicate that an improvement in this direction could indeed be attained, while further experiments 7 and 8 would indicate that attention should now be focused on a region around 7.

COMPLEX RESPONSE SURFACES

Because of the nature of the marketing "systems" underlying the sales and net profit response to many combinations of marketing expenditure, the response surface may frequently be more complex than the "simple" one illustrated by Fig. 8.2. This response-surface complexity importantly determines the kinds of experimental designs in marketing that are required to produce useful results.

Response surfaces not only may be frequently "attenuated" in the neighborhood of maxima as in Fig. 8.3a, but also "ridge" systems like that of Fig. 8.3b are possible occurrences [5]. One reason for the occurrence of such response surfaces is that the sales, or net profit response, of a product's marketing system will often be a function of the combination or interaction of two or more natural-expense variables. For example, increased sales of one product may be a function largely of more consumers becoming persuaded to switch brands. The most efficient market-

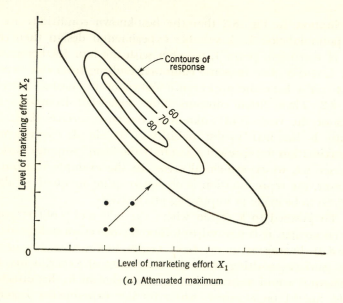

(a) Attenuated maximum

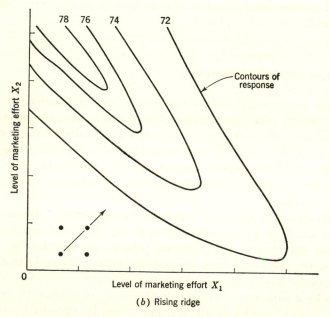

(b) Rising ridge

Fig. 8.3   Examples of more complex response surfaces.

ing "system" for accomplishing brand switching may be W, the combination, let us say, of increased advertising in TV (X_1), plus increased point-of-purchase displays (X_2). Thus, $W = X_1 X_2$, and $N = f(W)$. These ridge systems, in short, are associated with "interactions" between natural-expense variables.

If the experimenter did not know that the product's marketing system could most adequately be described in terms of the fundamental variable W, he might carry out experiments in which the natural-expense variables X_1 and X_2 were varied separately. But he would be ineffectively attempting to explore a system for which the response surface was like that shown in Fig. 8.3a or b.

Interactions between Variables

The detection of ridge systems of this sort is most important. When such systems exist, they provide both the experimenter and, more importantly, the marketing executive with a number of alternative combinations of marketing-effort variables which can be used to achieve the same sales and/or net profit response. Some of these combinations may be very much cheaper or more feasible or convenient than others.

Thus, it is often necessary to perform experiments with two or more marketing-effort factors simultaneously. Any experiment which attempts to avoid the multifactor or interaction condition by varying only one marketing-effort factor at a time will be almost valueless when the response surface contains a ridge, except possibly as a preliminary procedure. Accordingly, instead of natural-expense variables, it is frequently better to use the functional-cost groups (that are allocated by marketing-cost analysis techniques to individual products) as the individual variables or factors to experiment with as variants.

Experiments capable of determining how the fundamental (or functional-cost-group) factors jointly influence the sales and/or net profit response not only have the advantage that fewer experiments are required. More importantly, improvement in productivity can be obtained that could not have been secured by the one-variable-at-a-time method.*

* It is beyond the scope of this volume to deal at any length with the subject of experimental design. Several excellent books are available that treat the subject comprehensively. However, a variety of patterns of experi-

REFERENCES

1. John A. Howard and Harry V. Roberts, "Experimentation and Marketing Prediction," unpublished manuscript quoted in Ronald E. Frank, Alfred A. Kuehn, and William F. Mossy (eds.), *Quantitative Techniques in Marketing Analysis*, Richard D. Irwin, Inc., Homewood, Ill., 1962, pp. 49–52.
2. Seymour Banks, *Experimentation in Marketing*, McGraw-Hill Book Company, New York, 1964, chap. 1.
3. G. E. P. Box and K. B. Wilson, "On the Experimental Attainment of Optimum Conditions," *Journal of the Royal Statistical Society*, London, ser. B, vol. 13, no. 1, 1951.
4. G. E. P. Box, "Evolutionary Operation: A Method for Increasing Industrial Productivity," *Applied Statistics*, vol. 6, no. 2, 1957.
5. G. E. P. Box, "The Exploration and Exploitation of Response Surfaces: Some General Considerations and Examples," *Biometrics*, vol. 10, no. 1, 1954.
6. Victor Chew, (ed.), *Experimental Designs in Industry*, John Wiley & Sons, Inc., New York, 1958, pp. 138ff.

---

mental designs can be used to cope with difficulties such as those outlined in this chapter [6]. Among the most valuable are those based on two-level "factorial" designs with one or more added points at the center, reflecting existing levels of marketing effort. They have the following advantages:

1. They are relatively simple to understand, perform, and analyze.
2. The added center points allow continual reference to the standard marketing process and permit the cost in terms of "lost" sales, etc., of the experimental method to be determined.
3. Complexity of the response surface is easily detected by considering the relative magnitudes of the simple main effects on the one hand and the change in mean and interaction effects on the other hand.
4. They can be made the nucleus of more elaborate experimental designs, if necessary, by means of which complexity of the response surface may be elucidated.
5. They lend themselves conveniently to "blocking arrangements" whereby extraneous disturbances due to such uncontrolled variables as time trends may be reduced.
6. They can be adapted to the estimation of carry-over, or long-range effects, in experiments dealing with changes in the level of advertising expenditure or media strategy.

APPENDIX

DEFINITION OF COST TERMS*

Direct versus Indirect

A large proportion of marketing costs are indirect rather than direct costs. Direct costs are those which are incurred for and benefit a single segment of sales and therefore can be traced directly to specific customers, commodities, or other sales components. Indirect costs are those which are incurred for and benefit more than one segment of sales and therefore cannot be traced directly to specific products or customers.

Common versus Separable

Common costs are those which cannot, *as a practical matter,* be traced directly to specific customers, com-

* The material in this section is drawn from the author's *Distribution Cost Analysis,* U.S. Department of Commerce, Government Printing Office, Washington, 1946.

modities, or other sales components. Separable costs are those which can readily be traced to customers, commodities, and so on.

Whether a given outlay is a common or separable cost may depend on the circumstances of the business and on the segment of sales for which cost is being measured. If salesmen are paid on a salary basis, for example, the outlay for their wages is a common cost so far as individual commodities are concerned. On the other hand, if the salesmen work on a commission basis, the commissions paid are a separable cost of selling individual commodities, and they also are separable in regard to the cost of selling to individual customers.

In general, the greater proportion of marketing expenses are common costs, either because the process of tracing such costs to specific units of sales may be too expensive or, in some cases, because there may be no available method of making a practical and reasonably accurate separation.

Fixed versus Variable

The distinction between common and separable costs is related to another twofold classification of marketing expenses, namely, fixed and variable costs. Fixed costs may be defined as those which do not change in total amount when the sales volume is varied. Variable costs, on the other hand, are those which change in total amount as sales volume varies. The distinction between fixed and variable costs thus depends on the behavior of costs in relation to changes in sales volume. The distinction between fixed and variable costs is not a hard and fast one, but depends on the circumstances of the individual business and the particular segment of sales for which costs are being analyzed.

Thus, some fixed costs arise from a lack of flexibility in certain of the circumstances or factors under which the business operates. This lack of flexibility may be owing to sunk or irrecoverable expenditures, or it may be the result of contractual obligations assumed by the business. In other words, the amount of marketing activity or effort for which the cost is incurred may vary with changes in sales volume, but, owing to contractual obligations, the businessman cannot immediately make adjustments in the amount of the expense.

For example, the amount of delivery activity will vary with

changes in sales volume, but if a distributor who delivers by truck owns the trucks and pays his drivers on a weekly basis, most of his delivery expenses will be fixed costs in relation to changes in sales volume that do not necessitate changes in the number of trucks or drivers. On the other hand, if the distributor contracts with an outside firm for delivery on a zone-tonnage, package, or similar basis, his delivery expenses are a variable cost.

Similarly, if the distributor rents his warehouse or store on the usual basis of a fixed amount per annum, his rent is a fixed cost. However, if the distributor should have a percentage lease —in which the rental is a stated percentage of sales volume—his rent would be a variable expense.

Furthermore, practically all costs are fixed only within a certain range of sales volume and become variable when greater changes occur. If sales drop to a very low level, for example, branches may be closed or a smaller warehouse or store building rented, delivery trucks and other equipment may be sold, and policies with respect to retaining key workers and executives in the organization may be revised.

The permanency, as well as the range of change in sales volume, affects the distinction between fixed and variable costs. When a curtailment in sales is expected to be brief, the building, equipment, and organization will be kept intact, but when a long period of depression appears to have set in, expenses will be pared down. Conversely, when a sufficiently large gain in sales is expected to continue more or less permanently, an expansion of the scale of plant and organization to take care of this increased business will result in a rise in fixed costs.

This suggests that the proportions of fixed and variable costs in a given firm may change according to the time interval and the size of the segment of sales under analysis. In the long run and with respect to a large segment of sales, practically all costs may be classified as variable.

In the short run, however—as long as the "scale of plant" for making sales remains unchanged—and with reference to small changes in sales volume, most marketing expenses are in the nature of fixed costs. That is, small changes in sales volume can occur without appreciably affecting the aggregate amount of the distributor's expenses. For example, the net addition to the aggregate operating costs of a wholesaler or retailer as the result of making an additional sale are usually insignificant in amount.

The relationship between common and separable costs on the one hand and fixed and variable costs on the other can be readily seen. In the short run, and in relation to a small segment of sales volume, the separable, or direct, costs are mostly variable, while the common, or indirect, costs are, in general, fixed. In the longer run, the common, or indirect, costs tend to become variable.

Average versus Marginal

Another classification of costs is based on a distinction between marginal and average costs. Narrowly defined, the marginal unit cost is the increase in aggregate costs as output, that is, sales, is increased by one unit. The amount by which the aggregate costs increases is the cost of the additional unit. The average unit cost of any given output, on the other hand, is the aggregate cost divided by the number of units produced or sold. For example:

Number of units	Aggregate costs	Average cost per unit	Marginal cost per unit
10	$100.00	$10.00	. . . . .
11	104.50	9.50	$4.50
12	108.00	9.00	3.50

Escapable versus Nonescapable

A somewhat similar twofold classification distinguishes between escapable and nonescapable expenses. For example, if a single department in a department store were shut down, the expenses which could be saved would be escapable, while the remaining expenses of the store would be nonescapable. Thus, the escapable costs would be the same as the marginal costs, while the nonescapable costs would be equal to the aggregate costs after the department had been eliminated.

Imputed versus Outlay

For certain kinds of analysis, it is necessary to consider imputed costs as well as actual outlays. For example, a theoretical interest or rent might be charged to a commodity, even though no actual expenditures were made for these expenses. Such costs would be imputed costs as contrasted with actual outlays or expenditures.

Natural versus Functional

The ordinary expenses of a business (actual outlays) may be classified in several ways. The more usual method is on a so-called "natural" or object-of-expenditure basis. For example, rent and wages are natural-expense items. For purposes of analyzing distribution costs, it is found useful to reclassify the natural-expense items into functional-cost groups.

A functional-cost group is the cost of a single activity; thus, a functional classification puts together all the expense items that have been incurred for the same activity. A functional classification of expense facilitates the allocation of the common, or indirect, expense items, and permits distribution of an entire cost group by means of a single factor or basis of allocation.

INDEX

Date Due